AATSP

Professional Development Series
Handbook for Teachers K-16

D1520317

VOLUME 2
Teaching Spanish
with the Five C's:
A Blueprint
for Success

Gail Guntermann, Editor

HARCOURT COLLEGE PUBLISHERS

Fort Worth Philadelphia San Diego New York Orlando Austin San Antonio
Toronto Montreal London Sydney Tokyo

Publisher   Phyllis Dobbins
Developmental Editor's Name   Jason Krieger
Market Strategist   Kenneth S. Kasee
Project Manager   Tina Landman
Manager of Custom Production   Sue Dunaway
Production Manager   Lesley Kwan

AATSP Professional Development Handbook Series for Teachers K-16, Volume 2

Requests for permission to make copies of any part of the work should be mailed to:

Permissions Department
Harcourt, Inc.
6277 Sea Harbor Drive
Orlando, FL 32887-6777

Printed in the United States of America

0-03-077508-6

CONTENTS

INTRODUCTION

After years of public concern over the quality of American education, the 1990s were years dedicated to writing standards in all subject areas, both nationally and locally, with the goal of transforming the nation's classrooms into providers of a "world class" education as we approached the new millennium. For foreign languages, this reform movement brought inclusion in the core curriculum for the first time in recent history, and a challenge to determine what foreign language education was really all about: what should students know about and be able to do with the languages they studied? The question was especially difficult to answer given the historical lack of communication among the people who most obviously should address it—foreign language educators.

With the leadership of ACTFL and the executive officers of the individual language organizations (the "AATs"), a Foreign Language Collaborative was formed and a team of writers and a project director (June Phillips) were named. After three years of writing drafts that were reviewed periodically by the profession at large, the team produced the generic foreign language standards, *Standards for Foreign Language Learning: Preparing for the 21st Century*. They were presented to the profession at the ACTFL annual meeting of 1995 and published and disseminated in 1996.

The generic standards set the parameters for curriculum design, instruction, and assessments for the 21st century in FL education, yet there was a strongly felt need for language-specific standards as well, in order to provide examples that were clear enough for us to imagine what standards-based classes in the specific languages would look like. As a result, teams were named to tailor the generic standards to each of nine languages, and in 1999 *Standards for Foreign Language Learning in the 21st Century* was published, containing all ten documents in 474 pages.

The Spanish and Portuguese standards were written over a three-year period by sixteen Spanish and Portuguese educators representing all levels of instruction, including state and district coordinators and supervisors, as well as heritage language specialists. These standards maintain the five goal areas — the "Five C's" — and the standards themselves from the original document. They differ from the generic document in that:

- The introductory material discusses the status of Spanish and Portuguese in the world, the nation, and the schools and presents the unique case of Spanish for Native Speakers (SNS);
- Issues specific to teaching Spanish or Portuguese are raised in the introduction to each goal area and standard;
- The Progress Indicators are replete with examples of Hispanic/Luso-Brazilian linguistic and cultural phenomena, which are meant to provide guidance in curriculum development as well as classroom teaching;
- Thirteen learning scenarios specific to standards-oriented Spanish classrooms and five for Portuguese classrooms have been provided, in addition to those contained in the generic document;
- The Spanish- and Portuguese-specific standards extend to Grade 16, or graduation from the college level of study.

As the AATSP team wrote the Spanish and Portuguese standards, we were constantly aware of the need for further guidance for their comprehension and implementation, to the extent that we were tempted throughout the process to turn the project into a handbook for applying the standards to curriculum design, teaching, and assessment. Fully aware of the time involved in writing, revising, editing, and publishing two volumes, we often became impatient to get on with the handbook.

As soon as the standards themselves were completed, Lynn Sandstedt and the Executive Board of the AATSP named the editor and worked with me to design the format of the handbook, which was to be the second in a series of handbooks for teachers of Spanish. The first was *Spanish for Native Speakers*, published in early 2000[1]. Most of the chapters in this standards handbook have been written by members of the writing team of the Spanish standards.

The current volume, then, is meant to anticipate and address questions and concerns of foreign language educators as they work to implement the new standards. In it the authors point out the aspects of the current state of the art in language teaching that are already consonant with the standards, and they both delineate and demonstrate the changes that are necessary if we are to fully integrate the Five C's in learning and teaching Spanish, planning curricula and lessons, and assessing the results. In short, our purpose is to help to fill the gaps between the standards and what occurs in Spanish classrooms.

In this volume, we attempt to answer the following overriding questions, each of which is addressed in its own chapter:

1. How do you design a curriculum built upon the Spanish standards?

School districts nationwide have been grappling with this question, as teams of teachers gather to write curricula. Paul Sandrock and Donna Long, in the first two chapters, address the many aspects of this question. Sandrock outlines a process for designing curricula based on the standards, which clearly imply a broadened view of language learning and a more carefully integrated plan than we have seen before. He very aptly compares the standards to the four basic food groups, which are combined in many different ways to make varied recipes, just as the standards are meant to be integrated in such varied ways that they generate curricula that meet diverse local needs and preferences.

Mr. Sandrock describes the four possible reactions to the standards that were proposed earlier by Tom Welch, a member of the original foreign language standards writing team. He selects the fourth and most thorough of the four approaches, designing a curriculum "from the standards out," with "real life demands" at the hub, around which all of the components of the curriculum must revolve. He then explores each of these components, providing many illustrative examples, before outlining instructional decisions that are key to making the curriculum work.

Finally, he treats the questions of how to deal with multiple entry points and programs that begin at various grade levels; and he stresses that the process of developing a standards-based curriculum puts teachers and students in charge, not textbooks. Both Chapters 1 and 2 should help teachers to plan in such a way that the textbook becomes a resource, instead of serving as the curriculum.

2. How do you organize the content of the curriculum into a coherent but dynamic whole?

In Chapter 2, Donna Long outlines the many components of the standards-based Spanish curriculum and cooks up some sample recipes for combining them to create a coherent program that prepares students for life and work at the dawning of the new century. Giving numerous examples along the way, she clearly lays out the steps to follow, from selecting topics and brainstorming subtopics, to designing learning tasks and determining the requisite skills and linguistic knowledge for carrying them out. She then follows her own guidelines to weave together the many components into a sample curriculum for a hypothetical fourth-grade class, concluding with lists of tools for making assessments.

Finally, she provides four new learning scenarios (not published in the Standards volume) for grades 4, 8, 12, and 16 that illustrate how teachers can use varied classroom activities within a given topic, in order to address the goals and standards.

3.   How much does standards-based instruction differ from current practice?

Myriam Met begins Chapter 3 on a comforting note, letting us know that much of what we have been doing in line with the proficiency movement of the 1980s is viable for standards-based teaching. Communication in the real world is still at the heart of what the standards call for. Rather than start over 'from scratch,' we need to make adjustments to fit the expanded vision of our mission as expressed in the standards.

Met reviews current practices that can be retained, as well as ways in which standards-based instruction, as it is understood today, will vary from traditional teaching. She compares textbooks of yesterday and today with the more flexible instructional materials that are necessary for aligning teaching with the standards, giving students concrete, hands-on, personal experiences with the material to be learned.

She concludes the chapter by tracing the kinds of learning experiences that are appropriate for each age group—elementary, middle school, and high school—as they work within each of the five goal areas.

4. What are some ways to assess student progress in a standards-based program?

In Chapter 4, Greg Duncan begins by establishing some basic tenets of assessment today: it is performance based (it examines what students can *do*, not just what they know); it reflects the methods used to teach the material; and it measures progress in all five goal areas—Communication, Culture, Connections, Comparisons, and Communities.   Only through standards-based assessments will we know what our students can indeed *do* with the language. He leads the reader through an eight-step plan for developing standards-based assessments, designed to ensure that these guidelines are followed. He provides clear examples for each step.

Duncan stresses that without adequate performance assessments, students are not given an opportunity to demonstrate all that they can do with the language. Finally, he provides a list of resources for further information on performance-based assessments.

5. What is the role of the standards in teaching Spanish to heritage learners?

Ana Roca traces the history of Spanish instruction for native speakers, demonstrating that there has been a general lack of attention to the issue and a lack of understanding of the linguistic and cultural needs of these students. She then discusses the issues related to developing Spanish programs for the very diverse heritage learners, and points out several efforts in recent years to address these concerns, tracing the involvement of the AATSP, ACTFL, and various language centers in research and education.

Roca explores the ways in which each of the goal areas of the standards may be employed to improve instruction for heritage learners of Spanish, with examples, and concludes by describing an example of instruction that combines the standards for intermediate to advanced classes in Spanish for Native Speakers.

In two appendices, she provides lists of textbooks and other recommended readings.

6. How can technology be used to facilitate and enhance the implementation of the standards?

"Technology" is a broad term that evokes a sense of mystery and may still strike fear in the hearts of many language teachers because it requires a certain expertise with computer hardware and software, as well as competence with other machines such as those found in audio-visual language laboratories. In Chapter 6, Jean LeLoup brings technology within the reach of all of us by 1) defining it in terms of its many benefits to teachers, 2) pointing out how we have been using technologies all along in various forms, 3) listing and discussing numerous resources for teachers, 4) providing general guidelines for using technology, and 5) providing several examples of how individual technologies can be used in applying each of the standards to teaching. Additionally, we can all be encouraged by recognizing that all electronic technology experts are relatively new to this emerging field themselves; if they learned it, surely we can, too.

LeLoup explains the practical and theoretical bases for the use of technology in language instruction, and particularly for the implementation of the standards. She explores the applications of both Internet and non-Internet technologies. The possibilities for finding resources to meet the standards are immense, and LeLoup provides a wealth of suggestions.

7. What do the standards mean for post-secondary institutions?

In Chapter 7, Carmen Tesser and Frank Medley discuss the future of foreign language teaching in colleges and universities as viewed from the many perspectives represented among colleagues with diverse specializations: second language acquisition, literary studies, cultural studies, linguistics, and foreign language education. Their goal is to open communication among us all, to "foster connections and comparisons within our communities." The standards, implying an integrated curriculum, demand at least open dialogue. The standards motivate "an emerging common culture" within which we can better understand our own place in relation to others. Change is upon us, and "effective change will come only through collaboration."

The authors explore the challenges facing their two types of institutions: Ph.D. granting universities, and B.A. and M.A. granting departments. Until both become involved in implementing the standards, progress will be slow, since these institutions prepare future faculty as well as the nation's teachers. Faculty who have little or no interest will serve as obstacles rather than facilitators. The large Ph.D. granting institutions, which prepare the greatest numbers of faculty for all levels, may be the slowest to change. The authors point out that the catalysts for change will be literary scholars who invest themselves in the dialogue. They then outline five imperatives to which both types of institutions will have to respond if language learning is to be standards-driven.

To conclude the chapter, Medley and Tesser propose a plan of action for departments to follow in order to ensure successful, meaningful change—a plan that is already being implemented at one of their institutions.

8. What are the factors that will influence the degree to which the standards are implemented successfully?

Many times during the standards writing process, discussion digressed into the expression of concerns about the many educational and political variables that might affect the extent to which the "vision" underlying the standards would become reality. In Chapter 8, Martie Semmer addresses several of the issues that have not been discussed in depth in the other chapters. As she aptly states, "If foreign language educators do not lead toward the 'vision'…, no one else will."

The chapter is organized according to the various entities that have the power to effect or inhibit progress, from the diverse student population (ALL students are to become proficient according to their abilities), to teachers, school personnel, parents, official decision makers or policy makers, and professional organizations. In the process, Semmer dispels myths about language learning, proposes a set of competencies for teachers, lays out challenges for school systems, describes new opportunities for teachers to demonstrate their expertise, and calls us all to political action. She concludes with a model for program planning, to ensure adequate language instruction at the elementary level and smooth progression for students through a long sequence of foreign language study.

This volume concludes with a selected list of resources, many of which were suggested by the authors of the eight chapters. The list is not meant to be exhaustive by any means, but the books, articles, videos, web sites, and organizational addresses that have been included should provide Spanish teachers with resources for developing curricula, for classroom teaching, and for assessing student progress.

Although this volume is almost entirely devoted to the teaching of Spanish, much of what has been offered here is also applicable to Portuguese—indeed, to teaching any foreign language. We hope it will be of help to those teachers who are struggling with the questions listed above, just as the members of the writing team did—and still are, given the size and complexity of the venture and the evolving nature of the field of foreign language teaching.

Gail Guntermann
Arizona State University
Editor

NOTES

1. A previously published handbook, produced independently of this series in 1998 by National Textbook Co. under the auspices of the AATSP, is *Spanish and Portuguese for Business and the Professions*, eds. T. Bruce Fryer and Gail Guntermann.

WORKS CITED

American Association of Teachers of Spanish and Portuguese. *Spanish for Native Speakers*. AATSP Professional Development Series Handbook for Teachers K-16, Vol. 1. New York, NY: Harcourt College Publishers, 2000.

National Standards for Foreign Language Education Project. *Standards for Learning Foreign Languages: Preparing for the 21st Century*. Lawrence, KS: Allen, 1996.

_____. Standards for Learning Foreign Languages in the 21st Century. Lawrence, KS: Allen, 1999.

ACKNOWLEDGMENTS

A great debt of gratitude is owed to **Lynn Sandstedt,** Executive Director of the AATSP, for his outstanding leadership, hard work, and especially for his patience. The book would never have been conceived or completed without his leadership as well as the vision and selfless participation of all of the members of the Spanish and Portuguese standards writing team: **Donna Long, Frank Medley, and Carmen Tesser** (group leaders), and **Nancy Anderson, Rosario Cantú, José Díaz, Inés García, Nancy Humbach, Judith Liskin-Gasparro, Myriam Met, Marilyn Pavlik** (ex-oficio), **Alvaro Rodríguez, Paul Sandrock, Martha Semmer, Guadalupe Valdés,** and **Gail Guntermann** (Chair).

Many thanks are also due to **Peter Lafford** for his good work in turning the manuscript into camera-ready copy, and to our editors at Harcourt College Publishers, **Phyllis Dobbins** and **Tina Landman,** for their expert guidance.

1

CREATING A STANDARDS-BASED CURRICULUM

Paul Sandrock
Wisconsin Department of Public Instruction

In November 1995, language teachers cheered a document that represented major professional consensus around what we teach: *Standards for Foreign Language Learning: Preparing for the 21st Century* (National Standards in Foreign Language Education Project 1996). We quickly became familiar with and excited by the focus on five C's: communication, cultures, connections, comparisons, and communities. We found both comfort and challenge in the document as we began to implement the standards in our language programs in elementary schools, middle schools, and high schools. In November 1999, we received the next level of specificity: *Standards for Foreign Language Learning in the 21st Century* (National Standards...Project 1999). This follow-up document gave us a language-specific version of the standards and extended the five C's into the post-secondary level, showing us standards for instruction K-16.

The 1999 document itself describes best the effects on the profession that national standards were already having:

> Standards preparation is forcing attention to the broader view of second language study and competence: what should students know and be able to do—and how well? Clearly, the foreign language standards provide the broader, more complete rationale for foreign language education that we have sought for decades but never managed to capture in words or in concept until now." (15)

In our day-to-day teaching, however, we soon realized that this broad view was not sufficient by itself to focus student learning. A bridge from the standards to the classroom was necessary: *curriculum.*

How do standards and curriculum differ? How does a standards-based curriculum differ from a traditional curriculum?

While this document suggests the types of content and curricular experiences needed to enable students to achieve the standards, and supports the ideal of extended sequences of study, it does not describe specific course content, nor a recommended scope and sequence. (28)

Standards have broadened our sense of what it is we teach. Instead of just focusing on what facts and information we should teach our students, standards force us to state what is the essence of our discipline, that is, not just what students should know, but also what they should be able to do in order to say that they have learned a language. As standards show us the pathway for developing higher and higher levels of proficiency in using a language and entering a culture, we need to organize our instruction differently.

In fact, even the concept of curriculum has changed in this post-standards era. What used to be linear and sequential, now becomes spiral and more like a journey. Curriculum used to be a list of grammar and vocabulary, each assigned to a specific course where it was taught, or at least "covered." The degree to which students could use what was covered always caused frustration in both the students and their teachers.

During the development of standards in Wisconsin, my colleagues across disciplines shared several metaphors to help us understand what standards really are. One metaphor clearly described the relationship linking standards and curriculum: consider standards to be like the food groups. The chart showing the six basic food groups is a guide to good eating. A daily balance of the basic food groups will lead to better health. The description of the food groups does not lead to standardization of eating habits or minimal choices at grocery stores or restaurants. We have a variety of menus available to us, just as curriculum can vary. The food groups are interpreted through the specific context of the population being served. Specific purposes may lead to the food groups being creatively presented in a wide variety of ethnic menus. The food groups guide the choices in the daily, monthly, or yearlong menus we create and implement. The same applies to language learning, where standards guide our choices, but the curriculum needs to fit the context of the age of the learners, their interests and motivations, and any special focus such as a career or travel need. Even two teachers teaching the same course in the same school don't need to offer identical lessons day-to-day, if over time they are focused on the same overarching goals and work to prepare students to be able to do the same tasks in the target language.

Curriculum, then, can not just be a tightly prescribed series of content to teach; rather, it must focus on the end goals of the instruction, the actual student performances that will truly represent what it is to know another language. Knowing another language is not being able to fill in blanks on a worksheet, it is not identifying a series of dates. Knowing another language is having the knowledge AND skills to communicate, involving understanding and being understood, applying knowledge of the culture and the ways of functioning in a culture, and employing various strategies for effective communication. These performances and evaluation of these characteristics of knowing a language need to be captured in a curriculum, both for an entire program of instruction across many grade levels and also for each specific course.

HOW DO STANDARDS
CHANGE OUR VIEW OF CURRICULUM?

The Standards for Classical Language Learning (National Standards...Project 1999) explain what a standards document is *not*:

> It is not a curriculum for a Latin or Greek course; it is not a guide for daily lesson planning. *Standards for Classical Language Learning* does not mandate methodology; it is not textbook bound. It does not tell how to teach. It provides a destination, not a road map. (159)

Creating curriculum, then, is no small task; it is a journey. Curriculum should capture and communicate our beliefs as to what is the essence of what we teach. The essential components that will guide our instructional decisions need to be captured for ourselves; for our teaching colleagues; for the teachers of the levels/grades that follow; for our administrators to understand our focus, so that they can provide helpful feedback from classroom observations and in performance evaluations; for parents; and for students.

In designing a day's lesson, what goes through a teacher's mind? On what basis are the many decisions made? If you can turn to a curriculum that embodies the major goals for a course, and that clearly places those goals in the flow of an entire program's goals, then you will make sure that you are aimed at the correct target as you decide what students will need in the context of the current unit in order to show achievement of the year's goals. Without such a target, classroom decisions might be made on the basis of an activity that looks good, an exercise that worked last year, or an isolated piece of knowledge that needs to be checked off.

This does not mean that vocabulary and grammatical structures have no place in a standards-based curriculum; rather, they are placed in their proper role of supporting students' achievement of the performances described in the standards. They are not the goals of instruction; vocabulary and grammatical structures are tools that students manipulate with increasing accuracy, both linguistic and cultural, to achieve the purpose of communication as described in the standards. In my first years of teaching, if asked what I was teaching in a given week, I would have replied with a grammatical term such as object pronouns or the irregular forms of the preterite tense. Today, I would say I'm teaching interpersonal communication focused on strategies to dig for more information, using follow-up questions and rejoinders effectively. I would teach some vocabulary and some question formation, but my focus would be on how students were able to use them for a motivating purpose: interpersonal communication.

Curriculum, then, is the path described, the path to learning a language. Curriculum provides clear markers that lay out the route to follow as students progress in their use of a new language and their understanding of another culture. Curriculum gives the teacher the indicators that will help students chart their progress as language learners, indicators that are not just a list of vocabulary topics or grammar points, but functional goals that are both within reach and motivating in their challenge.

#2   WHAT IS THE RELATIONSHIP AMONG NATIONAL, STATE, AND LOCAL DOCUMENTS?

Standards for Classical Language Learning is a statement of what students should know and be able to do. State frameworks provide a curricular and programmatic context. District curriculum guides further define course content in a coordinated sequence. Lesson plans translate curriculum into meaningful and creative activities for the individual classroom." (National Standards...Project 1999, 159)

It is a question of specificity: The closer you get to the classroom, the more specific you need to be. National consensus created our broadest goals of the "Five C's." Our national standards tell us what students should learn (know and be able to do) and suggest how they might demonstrate that learning (progress indicators). State consensus adds more detail, especially in the area of *how well*—that is, a description of what level of proficiency is the target expectation at key points in a program. Often using our common terms of novice, intermediate, and pre-advanced or advanced, state standards or frameworks provide criteria for evaluating student progress along the broad path. State proficiency standards set performance at a level of specificity such as how well a novice student can describe his or her family and how well an intermediate student can tell a story (e.g., with lists or complete sentences, using very familiar words or a broader palette of vocabulary, and responding to well-rehearsed questions or more spontaneously). Local curriculum goes one step further and often describes the units of instruction, the thematic organization that will put all of these language goals and proficiency targets into practice. Local curriculum also shows the progress toward each of the broad goals for students to achieve in each course of the sequential program.

HOW DO THESE DOCUMENTS INTERACT IN THE DEVELOPMENT OF LOCAL CURRICULUM?

#3

Tom Welch, member of the original national K-12 foreign language standards task force, describes four local reactions that the task force found when visiting pilot sites during the development of the national standards. The four reactions provide four models for how standards may (or may not) influence local curriculum:

Reaction #1: Do nothing!

One local decision is to have nothing to do with national or state standards. A school may feel that it is doing quite well in preparing students for a future use of their language skill. Usually this is determined by looking at where graduating high school seniors are placed in the language program of the nearest large university. If their graduating students are placed into a fifth semester university program, it is logical to conclude that the program is doing its job. The district may not perceive any need to examine its program or compare its curriculum to national standards. One question to ask may be how many students are motivated to continue their language study through to their senior year and/or on into the university? If only a small percentage of students are in the final course in the school's Spanish or Portuguese sequence, the school may want to look at the broader view of content and measurement of progress that is represented in the standards. The standards specify course content and goals in terms of the purposes of language usage, which proves more motivating to most students who are less interested in linguistic analysis.

Another "do nothing" reaction would be to adopt whole-heartedly a state curriculum. Some state frameworks are fully standards-based and detailed enough to serve as local curriculum documents; many are not. Questions to ask before fully adopting a state document include:

- To what degree does the state document match the configuration of your local program? Does your district have courses that need to be filled in that are not described in the broader view?
- Is the state document specific enough to be useful to daily lesson planning, or will it end up "on the shelf"?
- Does the state document lead you to assess students in a way that matches your best assessment practices? Will you be gathering the type of evidence you feel is most valuable?
- Does the state document allow you to incorporate special needs or resources in the local context, such as a large number of heritage speakers or available community resources?

(New Jersey World Languages Curriculum Framework 1999, 36-7)

Reaction #2: Incorporate state/national standards into the local district's existing curriculum

In this reaction, the local district starts with what it has for a curriculum and overlays the standards when appropriate and/or convenient. The curriculum development or revision process begins with key units or pieces of content, often chapters in a textbook, on the left hand axis of a curriculum chart. Across the top are listed the five C's of the standards. The curriculum revision process is to check which standards are being addressed in each unit of instruction. On one level this is merely to create some degree of comfort. The local conversation might sound like this:

"In our foods unit we go to a local grocery store and restaurant, so we do Communities."
"Yes, and for Comparisons, we have the kids talk about what they eat for lunch vs. what kids in Guatemala eat for lunch."
"Oh, and we certainly cover Culture when we tell students that in Spain the evening meal occurs at 9:30 or later."

It is important to feel comfortable that we are doing some things right; however, the challenging nature of the standards would ask us to dig deeper and to see beyond what the teacher is covering, to examine carefully what students are held accountable to know and be able to do. The accountability in light of the purposes for language learning as described in the standards would be more than a true/false quiz on cultural facts. Students would need to apply their cultural knowledge in an integrated way to accomplish a communication task.

The positive effect of this reaction is that teachers begin to see holes in what they are currently doing and begin to look at their teaching through a new lens. Teachers will quickly identify that they are giving superficial or no attention to particular standards and will add something to their lesson plans. This is no small change in how we look at curriculum and let it impact our daily teaching!

Reaction #3: Correlate local curriculum to state or national standards

In this scenario, teachers are truly shifting their focus, from minimal to major impact on their teaching. The organizing principle for the course becomes the standards, which are used to determine content. The standards appear on the left axis of the curriculum chart, and the units of instruction appear across the top. Now the filter for determining content choices is the standards, rather than the text chapters or current curriculum (read "favorite") topics. Now all existing materials, resources, and units are carefully examined to see to what degree they support the achievement of the standards. Instead of measuring student achievement by the completion of a unit of instruction or a quiz on a piece of a chapter, student achievement is measured in terms of the performance standards. Students must show what they are able to do under the category of each standard as described for a given course.

Reaction #4: Design from the standards out

The most challenging approach is to simply use the standards as the basis for curriculum, creating the assessments that will tell the teacher and the student what evidence will indicate growth in learning the new language. Rather than relying on a text or teacher-controlled content to organize instruction, the focus would be on meaningful and motivating content through which students would develop language skill. Progress would be charted more closely in line with descriptions of proficiency such as the ACTFL K-12 Performance Guidelines. Students would be clear as to what they had to do to improve, what would be expected from each performance. Tom Welch says that this option changes assessment to focus "on the attainment of the standard at the agreed-upon level." Time would no longer be the constant; the standards would be, allowing students varying amounts of time to show their progress. The shift in focus is clearly to see the standards and their related assessment as the goal of instruction. When the curriculum captures that focus, it is no longer a linear list of content. This is a substantive change from the traditional development of curriculum.

WHAT ARE HELPFUL COMPONENTS IN A STANDARDS-BASED CURRICULUM?

Designing curriculum from the standards out resembles the image of a pinwheel. The demands of real life form the hub around which all the elements of the curriculum revolve. Each important decision of what to teach, of what to include in the curriculum, of what to assess, needs to be verified against the needs of communication in authentic contexts. This hub supplies the answer to students' most common question: why should I learn this stuff? The answer comes as we look through the lens of what achievement of these standards will help students do in real life.

Five components revolve around the hub of real life demands:

- Performance Standards
- Assessment
- Content
- Language Skills in Use
- Language Components

We will examine each of these components in detail, providing an example of what the curriculum might show for each one. The illustrative example will be related as a single strand of a seventh grade novice level Spanish curriculum.

Performance Standards

Answering the question of what students should know and be able to do, and how well, is the first key component of a standards-based curriculum. Performance standards come from national and state standards documents. They capture the goal for instruction and for assessment by describing the expected student performance. Performance standards combine the functional use and purpose of language with the targeted level of proficiency.

Example:

National Standards:

Interpersonal, Interpretive, Presentational communication

Culture—Practices, Comparisons between target culture and one's own

State Performance Standards: Novice Level

Students at the Novice level will:
Interpersonal communication: ask and answer questions
    Interpretive communication: understand spoken and written language that has strong visual support
    Presentational communication: write and present a short narrative about their personal lives

Local Performance Standards: Spanish-Grade 7

Students will:
Describe their daily activities
Read a simple paragraph on a familiar topic
Express likes and dislikes

Assessment

This element answers the question of how students will show achievement of the performance standards and captures how well students achieve these goals. The assessment needs to be specific enough to describe what students will do, but not so specific as to dictate only one possible performance. Rather than asking students to translate a paragraph or fill in blanks with specific vocabulary, they are asked to do something like describe their family. Different students will describe their family by using different words and structures; some may present their description in written form, others orally, some via video. Regardless of the mode used by the student, the teacher will be able to gauge each student's progress toward the goal. While there may be times that the teacher needs specific evidence of written vs. oral presentation, the more summative the assessment, the less restrictive it can be. Assessment must capture the essence of the curriculum, the key elements of the instruction, embodying what we truly believe is the most important component of what is taught. We need to ask ourselves constantly if our assessment is gathering the right kind of evidence of students' achievement of the curriculum goals.

Example:

Presentational Communication. Students present a description of themselves for the host family where they will be staying in Spain (oral, written, and/or video).

Interpersonal Communication. To prepare for the first night at their host family's home, students pair up and practice what the conversation might be like. They share photographs to describe themselves and their home and community. They ask each other questions about their lives (home, school, family, likes and dislikes). This is videotaped.

Interpretive Communication. To check their success, the students watch three of the videotaped conversations and write down all that they learned about the students in the videotape.

Content

This component focuses on the real language materials and situations that will engage students. Attention is given to connections with other subject areas and suggests the use of authentic texts and materials. A motivating theme could be the content choice for a unit of instruction, a theme which, like the language functions, has spiraled up from previous courses. The theme of family at a beginning level leads to an intermediate level discussion of what teenagers can and cannot do at home or at school, and ends at a more advanced level with debate over the roles of men and women in the target culture and the students' culture. The content focus may be a big question and routes for exploration of that question that will provide the context for the language learning and assessment.

Example: What students do in their free time in school, and expected chores at home; look at comparisons and contrasts across cultures and within American culture.

Language Skills in Use

This piece of the curriculum tells what specific skills need to be developed, clearly delineating the communication modes to be developed during the instructional unit (interpersonal, interpretive, and/or presentational).

Example:

Interpersonal Communication. Ask and answer questions, dig for further information in a conversation.

Presentational Communication. Clarity and precision in description, expanding descriptions with additional adjectives, phrases, or explanations (such as how something is used, when things are done, etc.).

Language Components

These are the language pieces that students need to know to be successful. In order to achieve the performance standards within the set content to be demonstrated through the described assessment, certain vocabulary and structures are needed. The standards-based curriculum provides key vocabulary areas and structures, not for their one and only exposure in the curriculum, but as pieces to be developed through the particular teaching unit. Rather than a curriculum that lists a grammatical structure once and assumes that students have learned it, a standards-based curriculum spirals structures over and over throughout a course and over the length of a program. The same is true for vocabulary, which is developed over time, rather than kept in unit-by-unit compartments.

Example:

Vocabulary of household tasks and free time activities
Use of adjectives to describe (form and position)
Question formation

The above written components of a curriculum provide a document to which a teacher can turn to plan her daily lessons. To put the curriculum into motion, however, three further instructional decisions are needed, just as the pinwheel needs wind to make it come to life:

- Applications
- Communicative interaction
- Guided Practice

Applications: What will motivate students?

Example: Bring in pen pal letters in which Spanish-speaking students describe their home and school life; ask for information about use of free time and household tasks through e-mail connections to sister classrooms.

Communicative interaction: How will students practice the language-in-use skills? What kinds of structured and unstructured activities in the classroom will help students prepare for the assessment that is the targeted goal for this instructional unit?

Example: Exchange information in class; have students describe photos from their homes; take students on a field trip of their school in which students ask questions in order to learn how to describe their school; teach expressions to ask for clarification and to elicit further information from classmates.

Guided practice: How will students learn the language components?

Example: Students re-apply colors in description to learn or review adjective form and position; apply description techniques with new words to describe photos from other cultures showing leisure activities; read stories (a day in the life of a young person) to add more vocabulary to talk about one's day or free time; apply formulas from stories to describe themselves.

In this development process, teachers create five written components of a curriculum that would help them decide what to do each day in class. The unit of instruction then becomes "Who Am I?" rather than "free time" or "Aztecs." The curriculum would set up clear performance standards, focused assessments, a content to explore that provides a context for the instruction, language-skills-in-use to describe specific communication goals, and language components providing necessary tools of vocabulary and grammatical structures to be introduced, re-entered, or mastered.

In the reality of implementing this curriculum design process, from the standards out, the unit of instruction will logically be thematic and related to the functional emphases of the performance standards. An overarching theme provides the unit of instruction. Realistically, students need some content focus, rather than simply a focus on a performance standard with unlimited context possibilities. In a classroom situation, students benefit from choices that are grouped under a common theme and performance goal, rather than without parameters. A theme could, however, embody a performance standard: Telling a Story, for example, would be a very rich "thematic" focus for a unit of instruction, allowing a lot of personal exploration by students around topics of their interest. Under a given theme, various standards come into play as appropriate emphases, not for their one and only moment of attention in that course or program, but as part of a spiral of recurring and improving achievement of each standard.

5

HOW DO K-12 STANDARDS
APPLY TO THE CURRICULUM OF
PROGRAMS WITH WIDELY VARYING LENGTHS?

This question confronts every district that does not have a K-12 language program. Configurations vary tremendously, some with multiple beginning points, some with only one or two beginning points. Variations include K-12, 4-12, 6-12, 3-4 + 7-12, 7-12, 9-12, 9-10 or 11-12—at least! The foreign language standards needed to be stated in terms of grades K-12 in order to share an equal place in the overall school curriculum with other subjects. Community members, when asked to describe the goals of a language program, usually describe high levels of proficiency in using the language. Such goals cannot realistically be achieved when students start in grade 9, or even in grade 6. The proficiency that the public wants from our programs is achieved by establishing clear performance goals for novice learners, appropriate for students in grades K-5; for intermediate learners, appropriate for students in grades 6-9; and for pre-advanced learners, appropriate for students in grades 10-12. This structure makes clear the tremendous investment of time that is necessary to achieve the high degree of language proficiency that people expect from our programs.

If a district does not begin its language instruction until middle school or senior high, the standards need to be adapted. Standards to be achieved by grade 4 can be interpreted as the first goals for a program, to help students complete the main competencies of novice learners. Standards to be achieved by grade 8 are a broad description of intermediate competencies. Each district can look at its program and determine when students achieve these basic competencies for the novice or intermediate levels. If it is determined that, for example, the grade 4/novice standards are achieved during grade 9 of the program that begins in grade 6, then the next set of grade 8/intermediate standards become the focus for the latter part of grade 9 through the grade where it is determined that these intermediate performances are achieved, say during grade 11. Then instruction in the latter portion of grade 11 and grade 12 can focus on the more advanced performances of the standards, knowing that students will not be able to fully achieve them. The standards, then, provide key program benchmarks, leaving to the local district the job of setting course goals to fill the spaces in between. The local curriculum will describe the performance standards achievable in a given course, knowing the amount of instructional time available. Numerous factors affect the real time toward proficiency of a given program model, including whether the schedule configuration is daily or every other day, or whether instruction is in a semester long block schedule or in a year long 50-minute period. Each course needs its own set of performance goals, representing expected progress students will make toward the broader summative goals of the standards.

WHO'S IN CHARGE OF THE CURRICULUM?

Traditionally, we have let textbooks control our curriculum. We either did it honestly, by simply making the table of contents our curriculum, or we fooled ourselves by independently writing a curriculum, which we then put on the shelf and picked up our textbook as the real driver of our instructional decisions. A textbook is by nature a more linear, sequential document, but learning a language is more a series of practices that come closer and closer to approximating the real life use of language. Textbook writers today would agree and ask teachers not to simply go through the text page by page. Textbook companies provide us with numerous materials and activities to help us select what best matches our students and our goals.

A standards-based approach puts teachers and students in charge of the curriculum and the learning. Teachers and students place the broad goals of the standards into a local context when creating the real curriculum. The goal of the standards is to bring into closer harmony the written curriculum, the taught curriculum, the tested curriculum, and the actually learned curriculum. Without standards-focused assessment at the core of the curriculum, it is very easy for curriculum, instruction, testing, and learning to be out of sync. Only a clear view through the lens of the standards will keep these components in harmony.

CONCLUSION

Are we prepared as current teachers to write such a standards-based curriculum, let alone to teach such a curriculum? It is my belief that all along we have wanted to operate this way. When a teacher sits down with a pile of papers to grade, there are gut-level beliefs that influence how she evaluates the student work. She has a sense of what she is expecting, of what represents great, acceptable, and unacceptable. Standards represent our consensus around those basic beliefs. Standards give teachers permission to teach toward those goals, being selective in content choices, opening up the ways in which students can show achievement of the curriculum goals. Instead of leading to a standardization or a limiting of options, standards allow teachers to be open to a broader spectrum of content and to individual student exploration of that content. This is challenging, but comes with a sense of comfort based on its similarity to our philosophical goals for learning languages. There is also both comfort and challenge in taking our familiar activities and content but adapting, dropping, or changing them in service to agreed-upon and assessable standards. Among language teachers there is a great sense of enthusiasm and energy around the standards, rather than resistance.

Are we preparing future teachers to implement such a curriculum? As teacher preparation programs help future teachers understand how students learn and in turn apply that knowledge to planning instruction, teachers will be better prepared to design instruction based on the bottom line goals rather than on a sequential content. Across the nation, teacher training is moving away from mere course requirements to accurate descriptions of the competencies required to be an effective teacher of languages. This is modeling a standards-based curriculum in the way that teachers are trained. This can only help as we prepare those students to be teachers ready to teach from the same perspective, focused on the bottom-line goals, and alert to the valid assessment of those standards.

Standards help teachers create a curriculum that is worth learning, by focusing on the essential skills and knowledge described as desired performances. The lens of the standards broadens content selection, opens up motivating options for students, and focuses instruction on preparing students to succeed in the performance that is captured in key assessments. Standards-based curriculum is motivating to the teacher and to the student. Both share a clear understanding of what is expected as a result of instruction and how it will be measured, embracing the curriculum because it is based on what is worth learning.

WORKS CITED

National Standards in Foreign Language Education Project. *Standards for Foreign Language Learning: Preparing for the 21st Century*. Lawrence, KS: Allen, 1996.

National Standards in Foreign Language Education Project. *Standards for Foreign Language Learning in the 21st Century*. Lawrence, KS: Allen, 1999.

New Jersey Department of Education. New Jersey World Languages
    Curriculum Framework.   Trenton, NJ, 1999.
    http://www.state.nj.us/njded/frameworks/worldlanguages

Sandrock, Paul. TEKS for LOTE Teacher Training Module III—
    Assessment. Southwest Educational Development Laboratory, Austin,
    TX, 1998.

Welch, Tom. "National Standards: How Will You Respond?" Presenter's
    Guide for Familiarization Workshop, *Standards for Foreign Language
    Learning: Preparing for the 21st Century.* Yonkers, NY: ACTFL, 1996.

2

CONTENT OF THE STANDARDS-BASED CURRICULUM

Donna Reseigh Long
The Ohio State University

The traditional curriculum in Spanish language education is organized around topics (family, food, and weather), linked with vocabulary clusters (family members, fruits and vegetables, weather expressions), grammar structures (*ser, gustar, hace* + weather expressions), and linguistic functions (greeting, requesting information, etc.). However, today's Spanish curriculum is increasingly viewed in terms of equipping learners with the skills they will need to meet their intellectual, social, and occupational needs. As the number of Hispanics in the United States increases, learners' opportunities for using Spanish outside the classroom also increase. Spanish-language television, radio, music, and print media outlets are now widespread, and Spanish-speaking associates are employed by many businesses. The opportunities and demands created by our modern socioeconomic environment call for creative curriculum planning. One midwestern university, for example, has answered a community need for bilingual health-care assistants by providing medical Spanish courses and internship experiences in local clinics. By using *Standards for Learning Spanish* (National Standards in Foreign Language Education Project 1999, 431-474) as an organizing framework for curriculum development, teachers can focus on higher-order thinking, such as analysis, synthesis, and evaluation, and incorporate the topics, skills, assessments, and outcomes that best meet the needs of their students.

CONTENT STANDARDS

Standards for Learning Spanish describes the content of instruction—what students should know and be able to do in grades four, eight, twelve, and sixteen. Like the generic *Standards for Foreign Language Learning* (National Standards...Project 1996), they are centered around five goals: communicating in Spanish, understanding Hispanic cultures, connecting with other disciplines and acquiring information, developing insights into the nature of language and cultures, and participating in Spanish-speaking communities at home and abroad. Standards set within each goal serve as guidelines for curriculum writers at the state and local levels. To these entities falls the responsibility for developing performance standards for learners and curricula to help achieve them.

The "weave" of curricular elements (National Standards...Project 1999, 33) provides a more detailed glimpse into the content of the curriculum and the integration of program elements. It depicts the interrelationships among the standards and the specific elements of the language learning program: the language system, cultural knowledge, communication strategies, critical thinking skills, learning strategies, content from other subject-matter areas, and technology. Each of these elements is treated briefly below.

The **language system** is comprised of many different elements, such as:

- vocabulary *(familia, actividades, comidas, salud...)*
- grammar structures *(pretérito, artículos, pronombres relativos...)*
- sound system *(pronunciación, entonación...)*
- alphabet *(ñ)*
- nonverbal communication *(gestos, lenguaje corporal...)*
- register *(coloquial, íntimo, formal...)*

Cultural knowledge includes knowing how to use the language system: knowing what to say when to whom and why. For example, students learn to use appropriate gestures, such as a handshake, *un abrazo*, or *un beso*, and both formal and informal oral expressions for greetings *(hola, buenos días, ¿Qué tal?)* and leave-takings *(hasta luego, adiós, ciao)*. Through this focus on culture, learners develop the understanding that behind the observable products and practices of a culture are underlying perspectives that determine perceptions and assumptions. Dale Lange provides a cogent analysis of the effects of the Culture Standards on cognitive and affective learning. Jan Gaston's approach to teaching culture takes learners through a four-stage process during which they develop cultural awareness and intercultural adjustment skills.

Communication strategies are an important component of the curriculum because they enable learners to interact with other speakers of Spanish. Some communicative strategies (such as agreeing before disagreeing: *sí, pero.../*yes, but...) may transfer from the learner's native language, but others (when to give *besos* y *abrazos*) will need to be taught explicitly. Some of the more widely taught communicative strategies include avoidance, word coinage, circumlocution, literal translation, language switch, appeal for assistance, and mime (Omaggio Hadley, 267-269).

Critical thinking skills have been a major interest of foreign language educators in recent years. Communicating in another language requires that learners be able to classify, synthesize, make judgments, and perform other higher order operations. Jane Harper and Madeleine Lively offer a number of TPR instructional units to teach higher-order thinking skills. And experiential language teaching techniques (Jerald and Clark) place students in situations similar to those encountered in the target culture and help them analyze what they have learned.

Learning strategies are closely related to the skills of listening, reading, speaking, and writing. Strategies like scanning for specific information when reading, organizing a written comparison point-by-point, and focusing on content words when listening, help learners to acquire and retain language. Like critical thinking skills and communication strategies, learning strategies are teachable (see, for example, O'Malley and Chamot).

A Standards-based curriculum also incorporates **content from other subject-matter areas.** By becoming familiar with the topics taught at the same level of instruction in other subject-matter areas, Spanish educators can reinforce the usefulness of knowing another language, as well as making lessons more relevant to the learners' experience. Of course, Spanish teachers are not expected to be familiar or comfortable with every subject taught in their schools, but collaboration with other teachers will enable them to pursue some of their own or their students' special interests. Ideas for making connections with other subject-matter areas can be found in most state curriculum guides. In Ohio, for example, fourth-grade language arts students study fiction and poetry and practice summarizing the texts orally and in writing (Ohio Department of Education). In the Spanish classroom, learners can explore similar topics by listening to and retelling age-appropriate stories or memorizing and reciting simple poems. Eighth graders study the historical period 1490-1815 in American history. By using computer software programs, they can produce multiple-tier timelines comparing significant events of the independence movements in the United States and Latin America. Further study of library and online materials could be used to produce poster sessions about *Héroes de la independencia.*

Technology has become a valuable asset in language learning. The Internet allows learners to experience virtual "travel" to Spanish-speaking countries and to access up-to-date cultural and linguistic information. E-mail, bulletin boards, and chat rooms permit communication among individuals around the globe. (See Chapter 6 of this volume for extensive treatment of the use of technology for teaching Spanish.)

PERFORMANCE STANDARDS

Standards for Learning Spanish (National Standards…Project 1999, 431-474) describe **what** should be learned in Spanish classrooms in the United States. Performance standards describe the linguistic performance of learners at various levels—in other words, **how well** they should perform. In the *ACTFL Performance Guidelines for K-12 Learners*, language performance descriptors are grouped around the domains of comprehensibility (how well the learner can be understood), comprehension (how well the learner understands), language control (accuracy of learner output), vocabulary (extent and applicability of the learner's vocabulary), cultural awareness (how the learner's cultural knowledge is reflected in language use), and communication strategies (how the learner manages communication). They also incorporate the three modes of communication detailed in the content standards: interpersonal, interpretive, and presentational. Guidelines are provided for novice, intermediate, and pre-advanced learners, at various levels of instruction. These standards provide a basis for designing authentic assessments of learner proficiency (see the ACTFL address in the resource list in the Appendix to order these *Guidelines*).

TOPICS

Traditional topics play an important role in the curriculum, not only because most textbooks are organized thematically, but because they provide a convenient framework for instruction. Countries or geographic regions are often linked with topics to provide a cultural framework. The following list of topics is as valid today as it was forty years ago:

- arts
- celebrations and holidays
- clothing

- environment
- family
- foods
- friends
- health
- housing
- leisure activities
- professions and occupations
- school
- shopping
- travel

In order to develop learning tasks, teachers can begin by brainstorming a list of subtopics related to each topic. A housing unit, for example, might include looking for an apartment, buying furnishings, finding roommates, designing a dream home, typical dwellings in a given country, comparing housing costs in the United States and a Spanish-speaking country, etc. After the desired subtopics are identified, specific tasks can be designed. "Furnishing an apartment," for example, might spawn the following activities:

- measuring rooms using the metic system and selecting adequately-sized furnishings
- selecting a color scheme and using catalogs to choose furnishings and accessories
- using adverbs of location and imperatives to tell "movers" where to place furniture
- searching classified advertisements to find bargains on used furniture; "calling" sellers for information not provided in the ad

When the learning tasks have been generated, each one must be analysed for requisite skills and knowledge. Telling movers where to place furniture, for example, incorporates the following linguistic elements. Representative examples are given for each.

- furniture vocabulary (nouns, adjectives, demonstratives): *la lámpara de cristal, la mesa de madera, ésa*
- commands: *coloque, mueva*
- adverbs and prepositional phrases of location: *aquí, al lado de…, en el centro, contra la pared*

• *gustar* and subjunctive mode: *no me gusta, prefiero que...*

Finally, grouping and oral or written medium must be taken into acount. Will students roleplay the task in small groups, or will they individually write instructions based on a diagram?

THE STANDARDS-BASED CURRICULUM: EXAMPLES

Like other curricula, a Standards-based curriculum must be articulated horizontally (within the same level) and vertically (across different levels). We might take a hypothetical fourth-grade curriculum as an example (Tables 1-6). As the tables show, the strands of the weave and the steps described in the previous section have been taken into consideration in designing the curriculum. For this sample curriculum, we have selected three topics—Family, Environment, and Celebrations—because of their relationship to other subjects in the fourth-grade curriculum. The tables outline the potential vocabulary, structures, standards, tasks, communicative modes, and assessments. The items listed in the vocabulary and structures sections (Tables 1-2) may reflect learners' previous knowledge, concepts and information to be reviewed, or new material that must be taught before learners are able to perform. The novice learner goals are based on the *ACTFL Performance Guidelines* for grades K-4. Learners who began their study of Spanish in kindergarten, who speak Spanish at home, or who have lived in a Spanish-speaking country may have reached the intermediate level or beyond by the time they are in the fourth grade. In such cases, the learners' linguistic proficiency will exceed the levels shown in Table 1.

Table 1. Lexical Content: Examples

Family	Environment	Celebrations
· members (*hermano, tía, abuelos*)	· geography (*Sudamérica, costa*)	· special occasions (*aniversario, día de santo, graduación*)
· personality traits (*simpático, extrovertida*)	· animals (*oso, gatos*)	· holidays (*Jánuka, Día de la amistad*)
· physical characteristics (*baja, rubio*)	· agricultural products (*soja, maíz, azúcar*)	· dates (*números, meses*)
· age relationships (*menor/mayor*)	· practices (*reciclar, proteger*)	· gifts (*flores, libros, bombones*)
etc.	· weather (*hace frío, tempestad, nieva*)	· typical sayings (*¡Felicidades!, muy amable, te invito*)
	etc.	etc.

These vocabulary clusters and examples are, of course, representative, rather than all inclusive. Many additional clusters could be generated for each topic.

Structural content that relates to the topics must also be specified in the curriculum. Again, the following table provides examples related to the topics of family, the evironment, and celebrations. If learners have not already acquired the requisite structures, they will have to be taught before learning tasks are assigned.

Table 2. Structural Content: Examples

Family	Environment	Celebrations
· ser/estar/hay (Hay tres personas en mi familia. Mi padre es de El Paso, Texas.) · diminutives (Luisita es mi prima. Mi hermanito se llama David.) · comparisons (Yo soy mayor que ella.) etc.	· infinitive used as noun (Reciclar papel es una manera de conservar los bosques.) · hace + weather (Hace calor en la costa.) · expressions (¡No tire basura!) etc.	· present indicative (Celebramos la Independencia el 16 de septiembre.) · indirect object pronouns (Les invito a la fiesta.) · commands (venga, no faltes, ponte) etc.

Relating the three sample topics to the Five Cs produces the following examples of appropriate learning tasks:

Table 3. The 5 Cs and Learning Tasks: Examples

Five Cs	Family	Environment	Celebrations
Communication (see Table 4)	Makes and describes own family tree; gives family nicknames	Describes environment of home state: geography, climate, agricultural products	Describes a typical Fourth of July celebration in the United States
Cultures	Investigates and reports average family size in a Spanish-speaking country	Investigates and reports contributions of migrant workers to economy of home state	Investigates how Independence Day is celebrated in a Spanish-speaking country

Five Cs	Family	Environment	Celebrations
Connections (Social Studies, Reading, and Mathematics)	Investigates Hispanic population of the United States and home state using demographic tables, pie charts, and maps	Uses Internet and other sources to find Spanish-speaking countries with which home state trades	Makes maps and charts to show independence movement in Latin America
Comparisons	Compares own family origins or immigration experience with immigration to United States from Spanish-speaking countries	Compares home state environment with that of a Spanish-speaking country that trades with home state	Charts dates of European encounter and independence for all countries in the Americas; compares length of independence movements
Communities	Interviews member of Latino community about his/her family's country of origin	Visits migrant labor service agencies in the community	Makes display about heroes of American independence for community center

Associated with the first C, Communication, are the three communicative modes: Interpersonal, Interpretive, and Presentational. Learning tasks should be created so that skills are developed in all three communicative modes.

Table 4.   Communicative Modes: Sample Tasks

Modes	Family	Environment	Celebrations
Interpersonal: Interacts with native speakers and other learners of Spanish	At a community center, a learner describes his/her family to a senior citizen.	In pairs, learners describe their favorite vacation location.	In a message to his/her keypal, a learner describes a party s/he attended.
Interpretive: Understands oral and written texts without recourse to negotiation of meaning	Learners read the Spanish version of *Hermanas* by Gary Paulsen.	Learners watch a video about the rain forest in Costa Rica.	Learners read about *el Día de los muertos en Janitzio.*
Presentational: Creates oral and written messages for an audience without recourse to negotiation of meaning	Learners present an original skit about a fictional family.	Learners write a public-service announce-ment about endangered animals.	Learners sing the song *América,* by *Los Tigres del Norte* at a Foreign Language Week convocation.

Assessments based on the *ACTFL Performance Guidelines for K-12 Learning* are used at regular intervals to evaluate how well learners use Spanish. Using the same three examples of family, the environment, and celebrations, we can examine several forms of authentic assessment for the Novice range. Learners' progress is assessed by means of products and performances beyond the sentence level and evaluated using appropriate rubrics (see Chapter 4 of this volume for an in-depth treatment of assessments).

Table 5. Proficiency Assessments for Novice Level: Examples of Tasks

Assessments	Family	Environment	Celebrations
Comprehensibility · give a simple oral description using familiar language · write a simple, brief, descriptive report	Describe family to class	Write a description of the Puerto Rican tree frog, *el coquí*	Sing *Las mañanitas* for a classmate's birthday
Comprehension · comprehend a simple face-to-face conversation with a native speaker on a familiar topic · comprehend an illustrated story for children on a familiar topic	Listen to a native speaker of Spanish speaking about his/her family	Read an illustrated version of a children's book about the rain forest	Watch a video about *La quinceañera*
Language control · most accurate when dealing with familiar topics using memorized vocabulary and structures · makes frequent errors in speech and writing	Write a paragraph about his/her family (*ser*, noun-Adjective Agreement)	Make a report about *el coquí* to the class (pronunciation)	Create an invitation to a party (spelling)

Table 5 *continued*

Assessments	Family	Environment	Celebrations
Vocabulary use · recognizes and uses everyday vocabulary related to familiar topics · uses words and phrases without awareness of grammatical structure · often uses L1 words and gestures to convey meaning	Describe a blended family	Use a map to descibe the topography of his/her state	Make a shopping list for a birthday party
Communication strategies · uses repetition and gesture to convey meaning · relies on background knowledge, nonverbal cues, visual aids, familiar language	Question a guest speaker about his/her family	Brainstorm suggestions for a school recycling campaign	Compare Halloween with *Día de los muertos*
Cultural awareness · imitates culturally-appropriate language and nonverbal behaviors · understands language that reflects cultural background similar to own	Greet others with handshake	Name animals that are endangered in the United States and Central America	Use gestures when describing a family celebration

Evidence of learning can take many different forms. Although we usually think of writing tasks and oral proficiency interviews as typical forms of assessment, there are a variety of procedures, documents and learner "products" that fit a Standards-based curriculum.

Table 6. Learner Products and Alternative Assessments

Learner "products"	Assessment formats
• brochures	• checklists
• charts	• evaluation forms
• compositions	• feedback from parents/guardians
• conversations	
• creative writing (poems, plays, stories)	• inventories
• displays	• logs
• e-mail messages	• multiple raters/panels
• forms completed	• narratives
• games	• observations
• interviews	• rating scales/rubrics
• journals	• reports
• logs	• self-assessments by learners
• maps	• tests
• oral presentations	
• role play	
• story boards	
• tape recordings	
• videotapes	
• visuals	
• web pages	
• worksheets	
• written reports	

ARTICULATION

The goal of articulation is a seamless progression in language acquisition from kindergarten through university. Taking Table 5 as an example, all fourth-grade Spanish classes within the same school district would study the same three topics and, ideally, use the same instructional materials for better articulation of vocabulary and structures. This would constitute horizontal articulation. Vertical articulation is achieved through a continuous spiraling and expansion of topics, vocabulary, structures, modes, with a gradual strengthening and expansion of skills through the various levels of study. Critical points of articulation would come at the end of grades four, eight, and twelve. At these junctures, skills and content knowledge of outgoing learners should match the expectations for incoming learners in the next higher grade. Actual achievement at each level, however, will depend on multiple factors, including:

- learner characteristics (aptitude, motivation)
- time on task
- quality of instruction (class size, equipment, facilities, teacher, instructional materials)

As a result, most Spanish programs are characterized by a wide range of learner proficiencies at each level, thus creating an articulation challenge. Some of the more common challenges to articulation include:

- programs that mix heritage and non-heritage learners in the same classes
- multiple levels in the same classroom
- large, multi-sectioned programs
- re-entry of learners from study abroad programs
- feeder schools using specific curricular approaches

In an attempt to address such challenges, some schools and universities have begun to instantiate proficiency requirements, rather than letter grades, as criteria for passage from one level to another (see Ballinger, et al.).

LEARNING SCENARIOS

According to *Standards for Foreign Language Learning* (National Standards...Project 1999), learning scenarios are "illustrative examples of teaching and learning which incorporate the standards" (p. 67). Scenarios contain a list of targeted standards followed by a description of the instructional activities. A "reflection" highlights the curricular elements of the "weave" represented in the scenario. Frequently, the scenario concludes with suggestions for extending or adapting the activities to other levels of instruction. The following learning scenarios, like those included in *Standards for Learning Spanish,* illustrate how various types of classroom activities may be used to address goals and standards within a particular topic. When developing activities, teachers can use the learning scenario format as the basis for planning instruction. The following checklist breaks the process of writing a learning scenario into logical steps which can then be combined into the typical scenario format:

- Specify topic
- Specify targeted standards
- Identify vocabulary clusters
- Identify requisite grammar structures
- Specify language skills to be practiced
- Identify linguistic functions to be practiced
- Identify supplementary resources
- Determine assessment formats and learner products
- Develop appropriate learning activities

The four learning scenarios that follow are further examples of the application of the standards in curriculum development at Grades 4, 8, 12, and 16. Like the learning scenarios included in *Standards for Learning Spanish,* they assume a continuous sequence of Spanish study; therefore, those who seek guidance for writing standards-based curricula can think of these examples as adaptable to various age groups of beginning, intermediate, and advanced learners. Brief suggestions are given in the Reflection sections for using the scenarios with other age groups and proficiency levels.

GRADE 4: *¿CÓMO ES TU FAMILIA?*

Targeted Standards:

1.1 Interpersonal communication
1.2 Interpretive communication
1.3 Presentational communication
4.1 Language comparisons
4.2 Cultural comparisons

Vocabulary: family members and related vocabulary, interrogatives, *ser, hay, llamarse, tener, más/menos*
Skills: speaking, writing
Functions: describing, asking questions, answering questions
Assessment: worksheet, pair work, oral presentation, composition

Fourth graders in Ms. Ruiz' class study the topic of "family" through a variety of materials and activities. First, they view labeled visuals and pronounce the words after their teacher. They also learn the terms *mayor* and *menor*. They practice writing the words by completing worksheets based on a fictitious family tree. Then students draw their own family trees, labeling the members with the correct Spanish words. Using the family tree as a visual aide, each learner describes his/her family to the class, correctly using the forms of *ser* and *llamarse* and *hay*, such as *Mi hermano menor se llama David.*

Working in pairs, learners ask about each other's family and practice questions like: *¿Cuántas personas hay en tu familia? ¿Dónde vive(n)? ¿Cuántos años tiene(n)?* Each pair writes a comparison of their families using *más/menos* constructions, such as *Daniela tiene tres hermanos. William tiene dos hermanos. Daniela tiene más hermanos que William.*

Using e-mail, each student sends a description of his/her family to a keypal in Chile and asks questions about the keypal's family. After allowing time for the keypals to reply, the whole class discusses the concept of *familia* as reflected by the members of their own class and their sister class in Chile. Using this information, they determine whether there are cultural differences between the United States and Chile or whether the differences noted in the families are individual only.

Reflection:

1.1 Students discuss their families with a partner.
1.2 Students read messages from their keypals.
1.3 Students describe their family trees for the whole class.
4.1 Students compare their families in writing.
4.2 Students compare their families with those of keypals in Chile.
5.1 Learners communicate with peers in Chile via Internet.

This scenario focuses on two goals, Communication and Comparisons. Within the Communication goal, students practice the three modes: interpersonal, interpretive, and presentational. They make linguistic, as well as cultural, comparisons. Linguistic functions include describing, asking questions, and answering questions. Both quantitative and qualitative assessments of proficiency are used. Older or more advanced learners may like to study famous families, such as *los Reyes Católicos* and their descendents.

GRADE 8: *AGRICULTURA EN MI ESTADO*

Targeted Standards:

1.1 Interpersonal communication
1.2 Interpretive communication
1.3 Presentational communication
2.1 Practices of culture
2.2 Products of culture
3.1 Making connections
3.2 Acquiring information
4.2 Cultural comparisons
5.1 School and community

> **Vocabulary:** animals, products, natural resources
> **Skills:** listening, speaking, reading, writing
> **Functions:** asking for information, creating with language, explaining, comparing and contrasting, persuading, reporting
> **Assessment:** lists, word game, poster, oral report, public service announcement, display

Mr. Delgados's eighth grade Spanish students studied a unit on *el medio ambiente*. In their social studies class, the students were learning about trade relationships between their state and other countries. Using the Internet, state departments of agriculture and trade, and library resources, the students determined which Spanish-speaking countries trade with their state.

Mr. Delgado divided the class into small groups, assigning each group one of the Spanish-speaking countries. The groups identified agricultural products from their state that are sold to the trade partner and agricultural products from the Spanish-speaking country that are sold to the United States. Using a Spanish-English dictionary, they found the names of the various products in Spanish and wrote original sentences incorporating each of the words/ phrases. They created a *crucigrama* or *buscapalabras* game based on the new vocabulary and included both the annotated word list and the game in a handout for the other members of the class.

Next, the small groups investigated farming practices in their assigned countries, noting similarities and differences to practices used in their own state. They prepared a poster illustrating their findings and used it as the basis for a short oral report to the class.

Finally, the students investigated cultural elements associated with agriculture in their assigned country. One group, for example, interviewed a member of the community about how the festival of San Isidro, patron saint of farmers, is celebrated in Mexico. Using their findings, they prepared a small guidebook describing the San Isidro festivities in a small Mexican town. Another group studied traditional cutting and plantation farming of endangered trees in Costa Rica. Then they designed a public service announcement about buying environmentally-friendly wood products. All of the projects developed by the students were displayed at their school's booth at a city-wide Foreign Language Day.

Reflection:

1.1 Students discuss agriculture in their home state and a Spanish-speaking country.

1.2 Students use the Internet and other resources to locate information about agricultural practices in Mexico and Costa Rica.

1.3 Students make posters and give oral reports to the whole class.

2.1 Students study the relationship between religious beliefs and agricultural practices.

2.3 Students study harvesting of traditional products and its effects on the environment.

3.1 Students use their knowledge of Spanish to learn about agriculture and trade.

3.2 Students interview members of the community about traditional practices.

4.2 Students compare agricultural practices and products grown in their home state with practices and products in a Spanish-speaking country.

5.1 Students interview community members to learn more about agriculture in Spanish speaking countries.

This scenario focuses on two goals, Connections and Cultures. Comparisons are primarily cultural in nature. Students practice all three communicative modes. Assessments of proficiency include: a game and a word list, group work, discussion, an oral report, and a public service announcement.   Younger learners, using age-appropriate resources, might focus on fewer aspects of this scenario, such as those related to deforestation in Costa Rica. Older learners could examine questions of ethics, preservation, and restoration of the environment.

GRADE 12: *EL HOMBRE CONTRA LA NATURALEZA*

Targeted standards:

1.1 Interpersonal communication
1.2 Interpretive communication
1.3 Presentational communication
4.2 Cultural comparisons

> **Vocabulary:** literary terminology, family
> **Skills:** reading, listening, speaking, writing
> **Functions:** asking for and giving information, analyzing, roleplaying
> **Assessment:** quiz, worksheet, class discussion, roleplay

In this instructional unit based on the short story *El hijo* by Horacio Quiroga, the students first participated in a brainstorming session on what it means to be "independent" in their own culture and environment. Then they answered the following questions: What are some of the uncertainties that face a newly-independent person? To what extent does an independent person maintain contact with family and friends? What are some of the manifestations of independence in your own culture (housing, source of income, car, etc.)? What constraints are placed on an independent person? When a teenager becomes independent, what expectations does the person's family have regarding contact with him or her? What continuing obligations does an independent family member have towards the rest of the family? A student "scribe" took notes on information provided by the members of the class.

As students read the short story, they looked for answers to at least three of the questions raised in the brainstorming session. After reading, the students discussed what happened in the story, and the relationship that existed between the father and son. Why was it so important that each keep his word? Is the story believable as presented by the author? Why or why not? In what ways does *la naturaleza* dictate the events that occur? How might the characters behave differently in view of the *naturaleza* that confronts them?

Working in pairs, students generated the conversation between father and son prior to the son's departure, and several pairs of students presented the dialogues to the rest of the class. Then students listed ways in which their own parents or guardians expected them to behave when they were outside of the home. They discussed what parents and guardians should worry about; what responsibilities students have to maintain contact with their parents and guardians when the young people are away from home; what other issues are raised by the story; what are some of the dangers that a newly-independent person faces when away from the family; in what ways where a person lives influences the ease or difficulty of becoming independent; and what are some of the reasons that a person might not want to become independent.

Finally, students prepared a roleplay version of an interaction between a parent/guardian and a child that reflected the realities of their own time, location, and culture. In order to avoid threats to personal values systems, they were encouraged to make the characters fictitious.

Reflection:

1.1 Students brainstorm details of the topic of the story and later discuss its contents.

1.2 Students read and interpret the story *El Hijo*.

1.3 Students present roleplays of the characters of the story, as well as characters representing their own time, location, and culture.

4.2 Students compare the actions and viewpoints of the story's characters to people in their own contexts.

The topic of this unit is most appropriate to the age level of those students who are contemplating leaving home and becoming independent for the first time. It would be appropriate for older students as well, as they reflect on the process that they are (or have been) experiencing.

Assessment stragegies included a quiz over the content (setting, characters, conflict, resolution, ending), which measure the extent to which students were able to read and understand the story on a literal level. A short composition on students' personal reactions to the story measured skill in self-expression and writing. Students completed a stylistics worksheet, in which they identified features of the story that the author used to influence the thinking/interpretation of the readers, such as the relationship between the father and son, expressions indicating the passage of time, and ways in which the author identifies the thoughts of the father.

GRADE 16: THE "OFFICIAL ENGLISH" MOVEMENT

Targeted Standards:

1.1 Interpersonal communication
1.2 Interpretive communication
1.3 Presentational communication
2.1 Practices of culture
3.1 Making connections
3.2 Acquiring information
4.2 Cultural comparisons
5.1 School and community

> **Vocabulary:** linguistics, legal terms, sociology
> **Skills:** listening, reading, writing, speaking
> **Functions:** asking for and giving information, narrating, summarizing, interviewing, debating
> **Assessments:** written summaries, oral reports, questioning

Students in a conversation and culture course that focuses on Hispanics in the United States learn about complex political and social issues, including the "Official English" movement, i.e, the effort to make English the offical language of communication in the states and in the nation as a whole. The course is designed for students whose Spanish is between the Intermediate Mid and Advanced levels of proficiency on the ACTFL scale.

Work on the topic began with students listening to a lecture by the instructor on the background, history, and current status of the Official English movement. Students then signed up for particular research tasks that the instructor had identified: history and current status of Official English legislation in various states, the roles of key figures in the movement, court cases dealing with language rights, and news items related to Official English. The instructor had put some of the readings on reserve in the library and, for sources she had found on the Internet, had either downloaded the material or provided the URLs on the course Web page. The instructor had selected research topics and readings that fit the proficiency levels (descriptive and narrative for lower proficiency, analytical and argumentative for higher proficiency) and interests (pre-law, history, linguistics, literature) of the class and gently steered students into appropriate areas.

Students orally presented the results of their research over two class periods, working together with the instructor to construct a fuller understanding of this complex issue. Each student also turned in to the instructor a written summary of the material that he or she had read.

The instructor had arranged with two Spanish-speaking individuals knowledgeable about the topic to visit the class—a professor of law and a graduate student in American Studies. In anticipation, students worked in groups to prepare questions for the speakers, and then formed one large group to review the questions of the small groups and select for each visitor a set of questions and a logical order to ask them. On the day of the visit, all students took responsibility for either one of the prepared questions or a spontaneous follow-up question. The class session was recorded on videotape, which was then placed on reserve in the Language Media Center.

For the next phase of the project, the students with higher-level proficiency prepared one-page position papers on an aspect of the Official English issue that had been raised during the discussion with the visitors. The students with lower proficiency watched the videotape and transcribed a 10-minute portion of it that was of greatest interest to them. In class, the instructor organized a debate on the Official English issue that involved the presentation of some of the position papers and participation by all students.

Reflection:

1.1 Students discuss the Offical English topic in class with each other, with the instructor, and with visitors.
1.2 Students read and react to material on the topic.
1.3 At various points, students present their ideas on the topic orally and in writing.
2.2 Students become aware of the multiple roles of language, a complex cultural practice, in public and private life, and learn how a cultural practice can become a political and social issue of considerable proportion.
3.2 Students bring to their work on the topic knowledge about the fields of history, political science, law, linguistics, and literature.
3.3 Students learn about the topic in Spanish from the instructor, guest speakers, and print and Internet sources.
5.1 Through reading about the experiences of bilingual individuals in the United Sates, students become aware of the different roles that the two languages may play in the lives of such individuals.

5.2 Through their readings, students learn about an issue that
    affects Hispanics in the United States.

This scenario addresses an issue of significance while also
helping students develop Advanced- or Superior-level oral
proficiency. The activities in the scenario are structured to serve
students whose Spanish may be at different levels. Students with a
variety of interests have the opportunity to capitalize on knowledge
and skills acquired through courses in other disciplines and to
acquire new information in those areas as well. Students also have
the opportunity to engage in a variety of speaking tasks—
description, narration, analysis, summary, interviewing, and
debate.

CONCLUSION

Using *Standards for Learning Spanish* (National Standards…Project
1999, 431-474) as an organizing principle facilitates the job of
curriculm specialists, as well as classroom teachers. The Standards
remind us of the important components of the curriculum, while
allowing flexibility within particular contexts. Most importantly,
the Standards reflect what is known at the present time about
language acquisition and learner characteristics, materials
development and learning contexts, assessment and articulation.
By using these *Standards for Learning Spanish*, prospective teachers,
administrators, textbook writers, and leaders in the profession can
influence the direction of Spanish instruction in the United States
and better help learners to appreciate Hispanic cultures while
acquiring proficiency in Spanish.

ACKNOWLEDGEMENTS

Thanks go to two colleagues for contributing the scenarios *El
hombre contra la naturaleza* (Frank W. Medley, Jr.) and *Official English*
(Judith Liskin-Gasparro).

WORKS CITED

American Council on the Teaching of Foreign Languages. *ACTFL Performance Guidelines for K-12 Learners.* Yonkers, NY: ACTFL, 1999.

Ballinger, Virginia S., Victoria E. Sherer, and Lisa Markovich. "Putting the Proficiency-Oriented Curriculum Into Practice." *Broadening the Frontiers of Foreign Language Education.* Ed. Gale K. Crouse. Report of the Central States Conference on the Teaching of Foreign Languages. Lincolnwood, IL: National Textbook Co, 1995. 124-138.

Gaston, Jan. *Cultural Awareness Teaching Techniques.* Brattleboro, VT: Pro Lingua Associates, 1992.

Hadley, Alice Omaggio. *Teaching Language in Context,* 2nd ed. Boston: Heinle & Heinle, 1993.

Harper, Jane, and Madeleine Lively. *HOTStuff for Teachers of Spanish,* 2nd ed. Arlington, TX: Harper and Lively Educational Services, 1991.

Jerald, Michael, and Raymond C. Clark. *Experiential Language Teaching Techniques,* 2nd ed. Brattleboro, VT: Pro Lingua Associates, 1994.

Lange, Dale L. "Planning for and Using the New National Culture Standards." *Foreign Language Standards: Linking Research, Theories, and Practice.* Eds. June K. Phillips and Robert M. Terry. ACTFL Foreign Language Education Series. Lincolnwood, IL: National Textbook Co., 1999. 57-120.

National Standards in Foreign Language Education Project. *Standards for Foreign Language Learning: Preparing for the 21st Century.* Lawrence, KS: Allen, 1996.

National Standards in Foreign Language Education Project. *Standards for Foreign Language Learning in the 21st Century.* Lawrence, KS: Allen, 1999.

Ohio Department of Education. Foreign Languages: Ohio's Model Competency-Based Program. Columbus, OH, 1996.

_____. Ohio Model Curriculum. Ohio Department of Education, 1999. http://k-6educators.about.com/education/ primseced/k-6educators/gi/dynamic/offsite.htm?

O'Malley, J. Michael, and Anna Uhl Chamot. *Learning Strategies in Second Language Acquisition.* New York: Cambridge University Press, 1990.

INSTRUCTION:
LINKING CURRICULUM AND ASSESSMENT
TO THE STANDARDS

Myriam Met
Montgomery County Public Schools
Rockville, Maryland

What does the standards-based classroom look like? What will teachers and students be doing and what will standards-based instruction be like when compared with current practice? The good news is that for Spanish teachers already comfortable with the instructional practices associated with proficiency-based foreign language programs, teaching to the standards is a natural next step. Many of the instructional strategies that have been associated with the proficiency movement will remain viable. Some will take on new or more significant aspects, while others may need to be revamped to align more closely with the vision of language learning embodied in the national standards.

The previous chapter described the content of a standards-driven curriculum. Standards are documents produced at the national or state level, and curriculum is a local specification of national or state standards, providing greater detail and description of what students should learn. In this chapter we will look at instruction, at what happens in classrooms to lead students to successful attainment of curriculum content and ultimately, national standards. Instruction is the important link between curriculum and standards in that it prepares students for successful performance. Instruction is also the link to assessment because assessment measures the effectiveness of instruction in terms of student learning: can students do what they are expected to do as identified in curriculum and standards? In this chapter we will focus on instruction by examining classroom experiences, tasks, and activities; on instructional materials for language learning; and on the interaction between the age of learners and the way instruction is designed.

BUILDING ON THE PRESENT

Before we discuss the standards-driven Spanish classroom, it may be helpful to describe proficiency-oriented practices that have characterized desirable instruction in recent years. Because the standards build on the tenets of communicative language teaching, it is likely that many of these desirable practices will continue to be useful to teachers as they align teaching with standards for student learning.

The primary goal of communicative language teaching is to prepare students to communicate successfully in the situations or contexts they are most likely to encounter. There is a presumed core of communicative needs that all learners may share: basic survival skills such as expressing personal wants; expressing likes, dislikes, and preferences; identifying and describing self and others; describing one's home, family, or possessions. Despite a shared core of communicative needs, there is also the assumption that learner needs will vary, that the preferences of one will not necessarily be those of another, that the skills needed to discuss a topic of intellectual interest to one student will be different from the skills needed by another for daily living in a household in a Spanish-speaking country. Thus, the notion that all students may learn some things in common yet also differ in what they learn has meant that the structure of classroom tasks and the kinds of instructional materials used provide for variability in communicative purposes.

If the goal of communicative language teaching is to prepare students for authentic language use in the real world, then it stands to reason that the organization of curriculum and instruction reflects those purposes. Whereas practices prior to the 1980s relied on a grammar scope and sequence to determine what was to be taught and how it was to be practiced, communicative language teaching has placed grammar at the service of communication. Since grammar is not the objective of language learning, but rather one of several means by which students achieve curriculum outcomes, grammar practice no longer has been the primary and central activity of classroom learning. That is not to say that students have not been learning or practicing grammar, but rather that grammar has been a component of classroom activities that build toward the focal point of learning: using language to communicate (Adair-Hauck, et al.; Lee & Van Patten).

Because the central aim of instruction has been to enable students to communicate, instructional practices have been dictated by the characteristics of real-life communication (Ellis; Hall; Hadley; Lee &

Van Patten; Shrum & Glisan). Classroom activities and tasks have been designed to ensure that there is an exchange of meaning. Meaningless rote exercises or pattern drills have been supplanted by tasks that require learners to attend to meaning—using language to say (orally or in writing) what they mean. Since in real-life all communication has a purpose (such as to give or get information, to express an opinion or preference, to persuade, or to socialize), so too, classroom tasks increasingly have been re-formulated from traditional practice to align with purposeful language use. Activities in which students have a reason for finding out information from a partner, for gathering opinions from classmates, for expressing preferences or persuading others to their point of view, bring language use in the classroom in line with students' purposes for communication beyond the classroom walls. Authentic learning activities are another instructional feature that parallels communication in the real world. Students should not practice using language in ways that are unlikely to be used outside the classroom; the materials they use should be drawn from, or at least simulate, those used by native speakers for similar purposes (such as getting sports results or reading for pleasure); the communicative tasks they carry out should be authentic to them (having 18 year olds describe an ideal mate vs. 8 year olds describe an ideal friend).

Pair and group work have become increasingly popular in Spanish classrooms. There has been a growing recognition that in real life settings, it is rare for twenty or more people to take turns communicating with a single individual. In real life, there is a give and take that most likely occurs in pairs or small groups. In addition, pair and group work have become a recognized means of improving student proficiency by providing more opportunities for language use in the classroom, thus providing additional support for the communicative goals of the curriculum (Doughty & Pica; Shrum & Glisan). Textbooks and other materials have broadened the opportunities for students to communicate in a number a ways. Many current textbooks are organized thematically around communicative contexts or topics. Non-print resources such as video provide access to language used by native speakers, and opportunities to see how language and culture are interwoven in authentic cultural settings.

In the communicative classroom, culture has been expanded beyond the traditional focus on the aesthetic contributions of the target culture, or its history and geography.   In proficiency instruction, the traditional culture curriculum (perhaps spelled with a 'C') has been augmented by an anthropological approach that encourages students to gain understanding of aspects of daily life, culture spelled with a 'c' (Hadley).

Because communication requires students to successfully integrate what they know into performance, communicative language teaching has required teachers to examine what students can *do* with language, rather than test exclusively what students *know about* language. The definition of 'testing' has therefore been seriously broadened to include a range of approaches to measuring student growth beyond those that simply involve paper and pencil (Liskin-Gasparro; Shrum and Glisan; and see Duncan, Chapter 4 in this volume).

With some exceptions (to be noted in the discussions that follow), much of what the profession has considered exemplary instruction continues to be valid in the standards-driven Spanish classroom. Teachers will not be abandoning the practices so carefully acquired and nurtured in the recent past, but rather they will be building on them as they align teaching to new standards for student learning.

In summary, the favored practices that will continue to be nurtured and expanded are:

- A focus on the communicative needs and purposes of students
- Grammar as a component of communication rather than an end itself
- Classroom activities that are meaningful, purposeful, and authentic
- Extensive opportunities for student engagement in communication during class, including pair and small group work
- An integration of many aspects of culture into language learning
- The use of authentic materials and commercially produced materials organized around communicative topics or situations
- Ways of measuring student learning that focus on performance, on knowledge in use

INSTRUCTIONAL PRACTICES IN THE STANDARDS-DRIVEN SPANISH CLASSROOM

National standards in Spanish and Portuguese are new on the scene. As a result, descriptions of classrooms aligned with standards are based on theoretical extensions of the philosophy underlying the standards. The recency of standards means that recommended practices have not as yet been validated to show their effectiveness in promoting student achievement of national standards. Thus, the following discussion explores what the standards-driven classroom might look like. Not surprisingly, much of the discussion will feel familiar to the well-informed teacher.

At the largest level of curriculum organization—the instructional unit—content will enable students to demonstrate understandings, skills, and proficiencies that are integrated and inter-related in terms of a given context, purpose, or situation. Units will be overall, 'big picture' projects or situations within which lessons provide learning opportunities for students to gain incrementally the skills and information needed to carry out the large scale task. For example, a unit might focus on a special occasion such as a birthday party. Students may be expected to extend, accept, or decline invitations in ways that are culturally appropriate for their age peers; they may need to know what takes place at a birthday party and how to communicate about that using elements of language (e.g., vocabulary, grammar). They may need to know how to read or write an invitation, or make a grocery list, or persuade others about the activities planned for the party and the kinds of music and decorations to be used. Individual lessons are designed to lead toward successful completion of sub-tasks such as extending invitations or planning party activities. Within these sub-tasks a variety of specific, discrete activities and tasks may be used to lead students to successful performance: vocabulary instruction and practice in pairs; grammar practice (e.g., " I'll bring...you can bring...Let's..."); examination of authentic invitations to identify appropriate language use; observation of oral interactions in which invitations are accepted and declined, to identify the cultural elements required for courtesy; practice in stating and defending opinions regarding types of music, etc. Cohesion from lesson to lesson and activity to activity within each lesson comes from an overarching purpose or context that determines what students need to know and be able to do.

In standards-driven instruction, major projects or units that determine day-to-day instruction will allow for the integration of all five goals (communication, cultures, connections, comparisons, and communities) as well as for the development of a range of language skills. No longer divided into listening, speaking, reading, and writing (and culture on Fridays), language skills are acquired to permit effective performance in interacting with others, interpreting what is heard or read, or expressing one's own ideas orally or in writing in non-interactive situations. For example, let's see how the modes of communication are involved when planning and giving a birthday party. To plan a party, students need to *interact* as a group, to make decisions, to persuade or dissuade, to exchange information or express preferences. They need to *interpret* written and aural texts such as grocery ads, party invitations, or TV broadcasts. They may need to *present* their ideas in written form — through letters or notes — or make lists. Students need to use their cultural knowledge to make suggestions when planning the party or to accept/decline invitations in socially acceptable ways.

Indeed, it is specifically in the area of culture that the traditional skills of listening, speaking, reading, and writing take on an expanded dimension in the standards-driven classroom (Klee). While language teachers have long acknowledged that learning another language is inextricably bound with learning another culture, classroom practices have not given adequate attention to the role that culture plays in conveying or interpreting meaning (Seelye). Clearly, knowing how to speak to a native speaker of Spanish requires some basic knowledge of courtesy in the language. In the past we have had students practice when to use *tú* or *usted*; we have taught the difference in the levels of politeness that are implied when making requests using the present vs. the subjunctive (e.g., *quiero* vs. *quisiera*, *¿puedes?* vs *¿pudieras?*). However, there are far more subtle and important kinds of information we have not focused on, even from the first day of class as we teach greetings. How important are greetings to native Spanish-speakers? How extended should the greeting be? When is it polite to switch from social greetings to task-oriented topics? While as Spanish teachers we have tried to help students avoid making grammatical errors — errors that in reality do not often interfere with establishing good relationships with native speakers of Spanish —, we have neglected the significant role that culture plays in how native speakers interpret what our students say to them. Indeed, a very small culture error can lead to serious interference with communication. In designing standards-based communicative, interactive tasks we will need to build in opportunities for students to practice more than words, that is, more than vocabulary or grammar, so that they also attend to the cultural aspects of their interactions (Byram; Fantini).

If cultural information is a key to successful interpersonal communication, it is even more vital when the opportunity for direct negotiation of meaning is absent. Successful listening and reading require use of extensive cultural knowledge for making accurate interpretations. Precisely because learners cannot negotiate meaning by directly asking questions of the speaker or writer, students need to bring to bear additional knowledge to the interpretive task. Students who read the Spanish equivalent of "Reds down Cards five to one" will find it meaningful only if they bring the necessary cultural knowledge to that message. Students will need to know that someone whom we would call a 'friend' in English is not necessarily someone who would be *un amigo* in Spanish, that in Spanish an *amigo* implies a much closer relationship. Knowing the difference between friend and *amigo* is critical to understanding correctly the implied relationship when the word is used by a Spanish speaker. Similarly, students will need to know the cultural information implicit in their style of written communication, their choice of words, or the ways they decide to address an audience if they want the message that is in their heads to be consistent with the one interpreted by a native listener or reader. At the higher levels of proficiency, such as those likely to be attained by heritage learners or students who have followed a long sequence of study, the culture embedded in language takes an increasingly vital role.

These cultural aspects of communication will need to be built into the tasks and activities students carry out in classrooms, and from the earliest level of language learning. Students will need to work with a variety of texts to gain interpretive skills, because text types and organization are highly influenced by culture. For example, although in the United States students are taught to look for the main idea in the topic sentence of a paragraph, they are not likely to find that organization typical of many expository texts in Spanish. Correct interpretation of tone of voice, facial expressions, and body language depends on cultural knowledge, and such interpretations need to be practiced by students exposed to a range of contexts and speakers that differ in gender, social status, or country of origin (Seelye). One implication for instruction is that a far greater role than ever before will need to be marked out for listening, reading, and viewing if we expect students to perform successfully in authentic situations when they leave the classroom. If we do not give students frequent access to such learning opportunities, they are not likely to attain the national standards we have worked so hard to set.

Not only will culture be integrated more closely with language learning, culture learning will take other forms as well. In the recent past we have done a very good job in helping our students acquire knowledge of other cultures, both in terms of big 'C' and little 'c'. Our students have been presented with many facts and information that have helped them function more effectively in other cultures or become more aware of the major contributions that the culture(s) of the Spanish speaking world have made. Because much of culture learning has been informational, transmission forms of instructional delivery have been common and quite adequate. Whether through readings, videos, or lectures, students have had access to culture learning in the classroom. As we move toward standards-driven instruction, much more of student learning will need to derive from inquiry processes facilitated by teachers rather than from information given by teachers.

Most salient in the conceptualization of the culture standards is the interplay among perspectives, products, and practices. Perspectives are the underlying attitudes, values, and beliefs that determine why people do what they do and how they do it. Perspectives determine (and may be determined by) customs, traditions, daily life patterns, aesthetic contributions, or the products used in daily life (whether fast food or cell phones). Far too little attention has been paid to cultural perspectives in the past, and for good reason. Many of us do not know the perspectives that shape some products and practices—indeed, perspectives may be implicitly understood but not explicitly known even by native speakers. Further, in discussing perspectives many teachers have been uncomfortable trying to explain the value systems of other cultures, particularly when they differ from our own. Moreover, discussions of attitudes, values, and beliefs may easily fall prey to stereotyping and over-generalization (Morain). It is far easier to clarify the definition of 'punctual' in another culture than to explain why.

It is unlikely that many of our reservations about teaching cultural perspectives will change dramatically in coming years. How, then, will standards-driven culture instruction manifest itself in classrooms? First and most importantly, teachers will need to ensure that students recognize that in every culture there are perspectives that determine products and practices. We may not always know them, be able to recognize or articulate them, or even discover them; but, they are always there (Rosenbusch). Knowing that every culture has a set of values and beliefs that shape cultural behaviors and practices is the first step in understanding other cultures.

Although some perspectives may not be known to teachers, some may be discovered through inquiry. Student projects that undertake to discover cultural perspectives are likely to be effective tools for discovering the *why* of culture. Research into the historical bases for customs, the attitudes of current native speakers, or the belief systems that generated certain products and practices can be carried out by students. Teachers are not the primary source of information but rather guides in helping students carry out projects of cultural discovery (Lange). Face-to-face, telephone, or electronic surveys are ways in which acquiring cultural perspectives can be blended with Goal 5/ Communities, allowing students to use authentic contacts with native speakers to learn culture. These kinds of culture projects will go beyond many of those currently found in Spanish classrooms where poster board displays proudly present information students have researched about countries or famous speakers of Spanish. Data collected from student surveys (who is the most important person in your life?), sample pages from numerous newspapers that provide evidence of the sports information wanted by readers, or statistical data (average length of annual vacation leave given to workers), provide authentic sources of information about what a culture or sub-culture values. Students will be active participants in creating their own understandings of cultural products, practices, and perspectives rather than digesters of information handed out by teachers.

Research projects will also be an effective tool for students to connect language and culture learning to the content of other disciplines. Particularly at the high school level, where students in any given Spanish class may be enrolled in a variety of social studies or science electives, it may be difficult for teachers to create interdisciplinary activities that link directly to subjects every student is currently studying. One avenue for making connections is independent projects in which students pursue topics of interest to them. Researching authentic primary resources will require that students use the interpretive skills as described in the Communication goal to access information accurately. Classrooms may look different from the traditional structure of twenty or more people focused on one individual giving out knowledge. Rather, classrooms may be centers of inquiry as students work on-line with the web, or use multimedia resources, video, or more traditional print resources to gather information. Pairs and small groups of students who share similar interests may work collaboratively on projects. For example, a pair of high school students studying the War of 1898 in their U.S. history class may compare newspaper accounts in the U.S. press with accounts of the same events in newspapers of the time published in Spain. Most importantly, as the results of student research are shared, teachers will join students as learners of new information accessed through Spanish.

For much of the last two decades, teachers have been encouraged to avoid the use of English in their classrooms. Clearly, comprehension skills can best be developed through extended opportunities to hear the language used in meaningful ways. Further, a strong belief in the role of comprehensible input has suggested many instructional practices derived from the Input Hypothesis (Krashen). If language is learned by matching what is heard with its meaning (comprehensible input) then it follows that the more one hears AND comprehends, the better the learning and the stronger the foundation for language production. While most teachers do advocate extensive use of Spanish in the classroom, there is no clear measure of 'extensive' use of Spanish or of the meaning of 'limited' use of English. In all likelihood, the current view of the role of English is likely to remain consistent, as will the ambiguity about the definitions of 'limited use.' However, in reviewing the cognitive demands that Goal 4/ Comparisons makes of students, as well as the deep understandings required for students to relate perspectives to products and practices, it may be necessary to re-think the place of English in Spanish classrooms. If students are to understand how their culture is just one of many options, and that the many cultures of Spanish-speaking countries represent additional options among the many, teachers and their low-proficiency students may need to use English to explore these concepts with deep understanding and intellectual rigor. Similarly, to examine the subtleties and nuances of cultural perspectives is complex and sophisticated, requiring more proficiency than the language skills most K-12 learners have at their disposal. For purposes of ensuring accurate understanding and deep conceptualization, English may be needed. That is not to suggest that English be used as the primary vehicle of classroom instruction, but it does suggest that English may not be banned from the classroom.

To summarize, instruction in the standards-based classroom builds on communicative language teaching, but may also differ from it, in the following ways:

- Standards and curriculum objectives emanate from the communicative needs of the learner;
- The five C's are integrated in each unit;
- Standards, curriculum, and instruction emphasize integrating knowledge into performance. Knowing about language is not enough. Students must actively use what they know in the act of communicating;
- Thematic or topical curriculum is organized into major units of instruction with lessons focused on sub-tasks and related activities;

- Units are built around projects or extended tasks; lessons, activities, and exercises build toward the ability to carry out the task;
- Communication is the primary goal, and use of instructional time is organized around communicative practice;
- Language learning is not built around the discrete skills of listening, speaking, reading, and writing but rather as types of communication: interpersonal, interpretive, and presentational;
- Classroom activities are meaningful, purposeful, and authentic;
- Grammar is at the service of communication, not at the center of the curriculum;
- Pair and group work are used to maximize opportunities to use language and to simulate appropriate intercultural interactions;
- Culture is more than big and little 'c', more than the aesthetic contributions or daily life patterns of the target culture;
- Culture is integrated with communication;
- Culture plays a much larger role in interpretive and presentational skills than previously acknowledged; students interact with a wider variety of texts and contexts;
- Understanding perspectives requires more focus on inquiry than on getting information from texts or the teacher;
- Culture learning and making connections with other disciplines are achieved through research projects, electronic communications, and other technologies;
- Performance assessments have an expanded role in that they provide more information about student learning than do paper and pencil tests.

INSTRUCTIONAL MATERIALS
IN THE STANDARDS-DRIVEN CLASSROOM

As was discussed in the previous section, new ways of teaching will require new or different instructional materials (Bartz & Keefe Singer; Hall; Phillips & Lafayette). These will be more than the traditional textbook and accompanying video; materials will include technologic resources, authentic sources of data, culturally accurate print and non-print materials, and interdisciplinary resources.

Traditionally, textbooks have been the driving force in determining what is taught and how. Textbooks and ancillary materials such as workbooks, audiotapes, video programs, and software have been integrated to provide a coherent approach to language development. Because the textbook has been, by and large, the core around which other materials are developed, the textbook has been the focal point of instruction and other materials 'ancillary' or 'auxilliary.' However, textbooks can capture only a fraction of what students need to learn. And, it is difficult to address the diversity of learners and their communicative needs in a single, hardbound text. If instruction is to align with the communicative needs of learners, flexibility in the material presented to students is needed. Similarly, assessments must be open-ended to accommodate a range of differences in what students have learned, even if all are held to the same content or performance standards. For example, it is likely that in a class of twenty or more students, there will be diverse preferences regarding use of leisure time. Not all students will need to express a dislike of skating or a preference for the ballet. Further, if quality instruction is responsive to the learner, then a fixed and static medium such as a hardbound book cannot be more than one tool among many in the extensive toolbox of instruction.

Oral and written texts presented through print, video, or other media need to include opportunities for students to observe, analyze, learn, and practice appropriate intercultural communication. Too often print materials written for students of Spanish (and not for native speakers) are written to practice language (vocabulary and grammar) and are culturally antiseptic. They lack the embedded cultural information that characterizes texts produced by and for native speakers. Whether video materials are instructional or drawn from the array of commercial entertainment products, teachers need to select materials that give students access to the cultural meanings of spoken language and non-verbal communication. And, because the cultures of the Spanish-speaking world vary, students will need contact with materials drawn from many regions and social groups.

If students are expected to make connections to other disciplines, materials must make content accessible to students who have limited language proficiency. By third grade and beyond, students are expected to use literacy as a tool for learning, recording, and reporting. Learners of Spanish probably will not have the sophisticated literacy tools at their disposal that they have in English. As the curriculum becomes increasingly abstract and reliant on verbal abstractions, the need for concrete experiences to access meanings will increase. Discussion of the causes of pollution in the environment is more likely to be successful in the Spanish classroom if students can call on graphic organizers, visuals, and concrete materials to understand the concepts or to communicate their own ideas. Thus, hands-on projects, concrete materials, and personal experience will play a greater role in the standards-driven classroom than previously.

In Chapter 6 of this volume, LeLoup makes a compelling case for the role of technology in the standards classroom. It would belabor the obvious to state here that technology is a critical material resource for teaching to the standards. Whether used for language practice, for communications beyond the classroom's borders, for researching archived information, or collecting data about perspectives, products, and practices of Spanish speakers, technology has extraordinary potential for revolutionizing instructional delivery and student learning. Most importantly, technology will place the student at the center of the learning process, and move teachers to a more appropriate role as planner and manager of the learning process.

IMPLICATIONS OF STANDARDS FOR INSTRUCTION ACROSS GRADE LEVELS

To this point, our discussion of the standards-driven classroom has not differentiated among elementary, middle, and high school levels. Indeed, much of what has been said thus far might apply to classrooms at all levels. The standards documents provide good examples of progress indicators that provide differentiation based on students' maturity and age as well as language proficiency. In this section we will explore some differences in designing instruction to align with standards that are dictated by students' cognitive, social, and psychological maturity as well as by the structure of schools themselves.

Goal 1: Communication

Appropriate goals and classroom activities for elementary school students will differ from those for older learners in a number of ways, for each of the communicative modes of the Standards—Interpretive, Interpersonal, and Presentational. Most young learners, particularly those under age 8, are still developing control over their native language. Their vocabulary continues to grow through schooling and into adulthood, while grammatical accuracy is fairly stable by the end of the elementary grades. Most elementary students are expected to master the fundamentals of reading by the end of grade 2; by grade 3 students are reading to learn instead of learning to read. The extent to which teachers focus on *interpreting* written texts with young learners will depend on the reading achievement of students. While students may be exposed to print early, they will not work deeply with text interpretation until the later grades. Keeping in mind our earlier discussion of the significant role that culture plays in the interpretive and presentational modes of communication, it is unlikely that teachers will give interpretive skills the same emphasis in the early grades as one might give to instructing older learners.

While elementary students are quite fluent in their use of oral language, the ability to tailor language to one's audience, and particularly, awareness of the subtleties of *interpersonal* communication is still developing. Most elementary students are accustomed to pair and group work, and are likely to stay engaged and on-task when working with partners on activities in Spanish, thereby gaining interpersonal skills through classroom interactions.

Like their elementary school counterparts, middle school students are willing participants in pair and group work. Early adolescents want and need to interact with classmates, since socialization with peers is a developmental characteristic of this age. Teachers can exploit early adolescents' natural interest in interaction by providing communicative, standards-driven tasks and activities. In addition, many early adolescents are reluctant to recite in whole-class activities or to make presentations in front of the class. For this reason, pair and group work becomes a welcome alternative that allows students to use language in a safe and sheltered setting.

Middle schoolers are increasingly aware of how speakers and writers shape their messages through language. As they develop reading skills in English, they are learning to analyze the author's craft, how authors use description or tension in character development, or how writers try to shape the reader's attitude through words and events. Working with a variety of texts, students discover how stance and perspective are important in constructing meaning from text. As school curricula increasingly include media literacy, middle and high school students can apply their viewing skills to authentic Spanish-language video to discover the ways in which interpersonal communication takes place among native speakers.

High school students can apply their English language literacy and literature skills to Spanish language texts. They are more able to analyze texts, oral and written, in terms of style and composition to note differences in the ways texts and communication are structured in English and Spanish.

Students who have completed a long sequence of standards-based instruction will be far more proficient than are today's high school students. Instruction for these students may be designed around the specialized interests or communicative needs they anticipate in future years. Students may be involved in setting goals for their own learning and creating the pathways to achieve them. Much individualized work will be carried out by students as they use technology and other resources to pursue independent lines of inquiry. Their research will probably take them well beyond the traditional fare of advanced high school classes, that is, beyond literature to explore topics such as social or political issues, economics, history, geography, or science in the target language.

Presentational skills include both oral and written communication. While students in the elementary through the high school years are ready to work on communicating through print, only more proficient students are likely to gain significant oral presentational skills. Yes, it is true that even young learners will recite poetry or fingerplays, but the more substantive communication skills required in the oral presentational mode depend on high levels of proficiency. Knowing how to address an audience (e.g., giving a speech or other oral presentation), that is, knowing how messages must be tailored to a specific audience, is a high level skill, and one that many learners do not even acquire in their native language until they have mastered the nuances of English.

Goal 2: Cultures and Goal 4: Comparisons

Most school districts in the United States include among their stated aims that students will develop an understanding of other cultures and skills in working with people of diverse backgrounds. Multicultural education includes the important ability to understand the perspectives of others, and to recognize how perspectives shape what people do or say (Morain). Students are also expected to see how their culture is one among many, and that cultures and languages may differ in other communities or geographic locations. Not surprisingly, these goals of multicultural education find a comfortable home in foreign language instruction.

For elementary school learners, cultural knowledge and understanding need to be consistent with their existing knowledge and skills, cognitive maturity, and social development. Young children have very limited explicit knowledge of their own culture beyond some salient customs, holidays, and traditions. They know little about geography and history, which influences what they are able to absorb and understand about the history and geography of Spanish-speaking countries. Students in the early grades are still developing the ability to understand that viewpoints differ, to understand the perspective of others. Because pre-adolescent children tend to be rather concrete in their thinking, instruction that teaches the relationships among perspectives, products, and practices will need to involve concrete materials, hands-on experiences, and many visuals. Simulated experiences in the target culture (e.g., riding the elevator and making sure you push the right button for the first floor [Curtain & Pesola]), or authentic encounters (e.g., guests to the classroom, keypals) are ways to link abstract cultural concepts with concrete experience, and help students compare their own culture with others. Teachers will find it helpful to align culture instruction with the concepts taught in the social studies curriculum, since that will ensure that culture instruction (content and methods) are developmentally appropriate.

By fourth or fifth grade, many students are ready to compare their own language to Spanish. They can discover commonalities in the Latin roots of both languages; they can observe word borrowings between the languages; and they can compare how the languages differ in the way they communicate information (e.g., *tener hambre* vs. to be hungry). By fifth grade students are learning about idioms, metaphors, and multiple meanings of words in English. Common expressions, idioms, or proverbs that are similar or different between Spanish and English can be compared.

Early adolescents are entering a period in which their peer group takes on utmost importance. Being like one's peers, conforming to the social norms of the group, is much more valued than is being different. This is an age when cultural differences may be greeted with laughter or feigned disbelief. Teachers of middle school students may find it helpful to focus on the shared human needs that are found in all cultures: the need for shelter, food, and clothing, for example (Morain; Seelye). Students can observe that all cultures have similar needs, even if these needs are met differently. Because young adolescents are drawn to engaging stories and exotic narratives (Egan), cultural understanding and perspectives may be effectively taught through authentic or fictionalized—and emotionally riveting—accounts of the experiences of Spanish-speaking adolescents elsewhere or even in their own communities.

High schoolers are emerging from the narrow focus of early adolescence, becoming more open to perspective-taking and differences among groups. A quick look in the lunchroom of any high school reveals the diversity of allegiances to a variety of adolescent sub-cultures—their norms of dress, speech, and behavior. The willingness to experiment with new identities and tolerate them in others is much more frequently encountered in high schools than in middle schools. The richer world knowledge that older adolescents bring to the foreign language classroom makes teaching about the products and practices of other cultures easier in that teachers can build on students' existing knowledge. Students are more able to pursue independent projects or topics of personal interest because they have developed the study habits and research skills that facilitate successful completion of these tasks.

Goal 3: Connections

Elementary schools are the place where cross-curricular connections are most easily made. First, the curriculum of the early grades has much in common with the material taught in beginning language study. Kindergarteners are learning to name the colors, to count, to identify quantities, to identify the days of the week. They learn about people who work in their community (police officers, fire fighters, dentists), they learn about families, they learn about themselves and their classmates. First graders learn about families around the world, they work with concrete materials to master concepts such as addition and subtraction, they measure classroom objects and their bodies, they talk about good health habits, and they learn to classify objects by their properties (color, size, shape, etc.). These concepts of the early grades curriculum can easily be taught or reinforced by the Spanish teacher (Met, "Learning Language through Content"). And because good elementary school teaching in general involves concrete experiences and hands-on materials, linking language with experience to provide comprehensible input is facilitated for the Spanish teacher. Connections between the Spanish curriculum and instruction in the regular curriculum are also made easier by the self-contained nature of most elementary school classrooms. Most students spend the overwhelming majority of their school day with the same teacher and classmates. Collaboration between teachers is facilitated simply because there are fewer people who need to meet and work together, and because all students are learning the same content material.

Middle schoolers, like their elementary school counterparts, are likely to spend a good part of their day with the same classmates. As a result, almost all students in the Spanish class are also learning the same content in other disciplines. There is only one social studies course to connect with, only one curriculum for grade 7 reading (even if students vary in achievement levels), only one science that most 6th graders take. Decisions about connections to other disciplines are likely to benefit all students. Although middle schoolers may see several teachers each day, Spanish teachers will benefit from the prevailing organization of middle schools into teams. Most schools assign students to a team of teachers, drawing one teacher from each of the major content areas students are studying. Teams often plan together, developing interdisciplinary thematic units that connect the content of subject areas to one another. In these settings, Spanish teachers will find collaboration with a team already focused on making connections facilitated by the organization and philosophy of the middle school.

In high schools, connections are more likely to be made by the individual Spanish teacher selecting level-appropriate content through which language may be learned or practiced. For example, a unit on clothing can connect with mathematics as students calculate the final prices of garments, applying discounts and taxes as appropriate. Students can compare the density of urban and rural populations in regions of Africa while practicing comparatives, superlatives, *más de* (vs. *que*), or structures such as *tantos... como*. They can practice weather vocabulary while comparing and contrasting the differential effects of *El Niño* or *La Niña*. Decisions about connections to be made between the Spanish curriculum and other areas are made by the teacher (Met, "Making Connections").

In contrast, other kinds of decisions about content connections can be made by students. Students fascinated by medieval history may read texts or do research projects. These students are likely to develop better reading skills and internalize forms of the past tense. Other students may be interested in social issues, and interview members of the local community in Spanish to collect data about community attitudes and perspectives. Compared to the students researching life in medieval times, these students are more likely to gain increased proficiency in interpersonal communication and gain greater sensitivity to the cultural meanings inherent in language use. Classrooms in which connections are made primarily through independent study will look different because the dominant form of classroom structure will be students working individually or in small groups.

Goal 5: Communities

Standards-driven instruction should allow all students to use Spanish to communicate beyond the walls of the classroom or school. At any age, students in many communities are already able to interact with school mates who come to school already knowing how to speak Spanish. Many elementary schools already have computer access—in media centers, computer labs, or even in classrooms—that allow students to communicate electronically with keypals or access information on the worldwide web. Middle schools are even more likely to have electronic access, and high schools are most likely of all to allow students to use Spanish to interact electronically with communities both within and beyond the local area. High school students may have additional opportunities to use Spanish in their community through extra-curricular activities, part-time or summer jobs, and even travel. While elementary school projects that involve interacting with local communities may be undertaken as a whole class or through field trips, high schoolers may complete research projects by collecting data, administering surveys, or conducting interviews. Middle and high school students can be encouraged to fulfill community service requirements by volunteering to assist Spanish speaking students within the school or working in volunteer assignments in the local community. Although the age and maturity of students may set some parameters on the types of community engagement that teachers plan, students of all ages can and should use Spanish as feasible in their local setting or in the global community.

CONCLUSION

What does the standards-driven classroom look like? How is instruction delivered? How do teachers help students learn? To be honest, in many ways, the standards-based classroom doesn't look very different from exemplary classrooms in the very recent past. The goal of instruction is communication. Instruction prepares students for successful real-life uses of Spanish. It enables students to interact appropriately with comfort and fluency, with increasing degrees of grammatical accuracy, and with intercultural appropriateness. Practice activities reflect the characteristics of real-life communication: students interact with peers, they interpret aural and written texts, they write to communicate their own thoughts to others.

Where standards-based classrooms differ is primarily in areas of emphasis and organization. The 'four skills' are no longer discrete aspects of performance. Rather, three modes of communication determine the kinds of skills students need (interpersonal, interpretive, and presentational). The emphasis given to accuracy in the past is broadened or modified to give greater attention to cultural 'accuracy.' Culture is no longer divided between traditional culture topics and the daily life patterns of the culture. Rather, both are woven into a framework that views the products of cultures (the arts, literature, common household furnishings, and foods) and the practices of cultures (customs, traditions, and day-to-day life styles) as mutually influencing and influenced by cultural perspectives (attitudes, values, and belief systems). Fridays will no longer be culture day; every day will be culture day if we teach to the standards.

Standards-based instruction builds on the recent past; we will not throw out the baby with the bathwater. By the same token, it is important to recognize that teaching will be different and many new challenges await us. Over the last decades, instructional repertoires were expanded, refined, and validated to be consistent with the philosophy and objectives of communicative language teaching. In the coming years, we will need to expand our current repertoires, develop new approaches, and validate their effectiveness as we move national standards from a paper document to an enriching learning experience in every classroom for every student, every day.

WORKS CITED

Adair-Hauck, Bonnie, Richard Donato, and Philomena Cumo. "Using a Whole Language Approach to Teach Grammar." *Teacher's Handbook. Contextualized Language Instruction.* Eds. Judith Shrum and Eileen Glisan. Boston: Heinle & Heinle Publishers, 1994. 90-111.

Bartz, Walter, and Margaret Keefe Singer. "The Programmatic Implications of Foreign Language Standards." *National Standards. A Catalyst for Reform.* Ed. Robert Lafayette. Lincolnwood, IL: National Textbook Co., 1996. 139-167.

Byram, Michael. *Teaching and Assessing Intercultural Competence.* Clevedon, U.K.: Multilingual Matters, 1997.

Curtain, Helena A., and Carol Ann Pesola. *Languages And Children: Making The Match.* New York: Longman, 1994.

Doughty, Catherine, and Teresa Pica. "'Information Gap' Tasks: Do They Facilitate Second Language Acquisition?" *TESOL Quarterly* 20 (1986): 305-325.

Ellis, Rod. *Instructed Language Acquisition.* Oxford, U.K.: Blackwell Publishers, 1990.

Egan, Kieran. *Imagination in Teaching and Learning. The Middle School Years.* Chicago, IL: University of Chicago Press, 1992.

Fantini, Alvino. "Comparisons: towards the Development of Intercultural Competence." *Foreign Language Standards: Linking Theory, Research, and Practice.* Ed. June K. Phillips. Lincolnwood, IL: National Textbook Co., 1999. 165-218.

Hadley, Alice Omaggio. *Teaching Language in Context,* 2nd ed. Boston: Heinle & Heinle Publishers, 1993.

Hall, Joan Kelly. "The Communication Standards." *Foreign Language Standards: Linking Theory, Research, and Practice.* Ed. June K. Phillips. Lincolnwood, IL: National Textbook Co., 1999. 15-56.

Klee, Carol A. "Communication as an Organizaing Principle in the National Standards: Sociolinguistic Aspects of Spanish Language Teaching." *Hispania* 81 (1998): 339-351.

Krashen, Stephen. Principles and Practice in Second Language Acquisition. Oxford: Pergamon Press, 1982.

Lange, Dale. "Planning for and Using the New National Culture Standards." *Foreign Language Standards: Linking Theory, Research, and Practice.* Ed. June K. Phillips. Lincolnwood, IL: National Textbook Co., 1999. 57-136.

Lee, James, and Bill Van Patten. *Making Communicative LanguageTeaching Happen.* New York: Mc Graw Hill, 1995.

Liskin-Gasparro, Judith. "Assessment: From Content Standards to Student Performance." *National Standards. A Catalyst for Reform.* Ed. Robert C. Lafayette. Lincolnwood, IL: National Textbook Co., 1996. 169-96.

Met, Myriam. "Learning Language Through Content: Learning Content Through Language." *Foreign Language Annals* 24 (1991): 281-295.

_____. "Making Connections." *Foreign Language Standards: Linking Theory, Research, and Practice.* Ed. June K. Phillips. Lincolnwood, IL: National Textbook Co., 1999. 137-64.

Morain, Genelle. "Teaching for Cultural Diversity." *Research Within Reach II.* Eds. Carol Herron and Vicki Galloway. Valdosta, GA: Southern Conference on Language Teaching, 1995. 43-60.

Phillips, June K., and Robert C. Lafayette. "Reactions to the Catalyst: Implications for Our New Professional Structure." *National Standards. A Catalyst for Reform.* Ed. Robert C. Lafayette. Lincolnwood, IL: National Textbook Co., 1996. 197-209.

Rosenbusch, Marcia, ed. *Bringing the Standards into the Classroom: A Teacher's Guide.* Ames, IA: National K-12 Foreign Language Resource Center, Iowa State University, 1997.

Seelye, H. Ned. *Teaching Culture* (3rd ed.). Lincolnwood, IL: National Textbook Co., 1993.

Shrum, Judith, and Eileen Glisan. *Teacher's Handbook. Contextualized Language Instruction.* Boston: Heinle & Heinle Publishers, 1994.

4

THE STANDARDS-BASED CLASSROOM
AND ASSESSMENT:
THE PROOF IS IN THE PUDDING

Greg Duncan
InterPrep, Inc.

As the 21st century begins, American foreign language educators possess more knowledge and more tools than ever before, to make it possible to provide the finest foreign language programs available anywhere on the globe. In addition to a growing research base on good practice, the profession has amassed products such as *Standards for Foreign Language Learning in the 21st Century* (National Standards in Foreign Language Education Project 1999) and the *ACTFL Performance Guidelines for K-12 Learners* (American Council on the Teaching of Foreign Languages 1999), which provide direct classroom assistance in preparing students for functional language ability. Accompanying these pedagogical advances, educators are experiencing unparalleled interest, support and even pressure from the public and policy makers to make certain that American students are capable of competing in an ever increasing global marketplace.

These positive factors have all created a strong impact on learning foreign languages in our nation's classrooms, where emphasis is predominantly placed on using the language as opposed to studying about it. An unfortunate disconnect in this promising picture is the lack of consonance often found between instructional priorities and assessment practices. While the classroom environment looks increasingly performance-based, the assessment environment is still often dominated by paper-and-pencil measurements confined to assessing what students know, not what they can *do*. This chapter addresses this problem by suggesting an eight-step plan that teachers can follow to ensure not only that students are assessed on what they learned, but that the methods used to assess students' language performance abilities mirror those used to instruct them.

DETERMINING WHAT TO ASSESS

Every well-trained educator knows that the first step in a good assessment plan is specifying what it is that one wants to assess. While this statement may sound obvious to the point of being ridiculous, identifying the content to be assessed is not always easy or unanimously agreed upon by professional educators, and foreign language education is no exception to this phenomenon. For decades, foreign language educators at local and state levels determined, to the best of their knowledge and abilities, what was taught and subsequently assessed. There existed no national consensus regarding *what* should be taught *to whom* and *by when*.

Fortunately, 1996 brought a whole new way of viewing language learning, teaching and assessment, with the release of national standards for foreign languages (National Standards...Project 1996). These standards, developed over a three-year period, 1) represent the best thinking of some of the profession's brightest and best minds, 2) reflect the collective thoughts of all American foreign language educators as the result of a comprehensive and open review process, 3) set a vision of what foreign language educators think *ought to be* the goals to work toward, and 4) serve as a frame from which states and local school districts can construct more specific goals and learner outcomes.

The generic standards, released in 1996 under the title *Standards for Foreign Language Learning: Preparing for the 21st Century*, served as the inspiration for publication of a yet more comprehensive document in 1999 that makes language-specific standards available in nine different languages. *Standards for Foreign Language Learning in the 21st Century* not only includes the generic goals and standards that apply to the teaching of all foreign languages, it also provides language-specific standards, complete with language-specific learning scenarios, for Chinese, Classical Languages, French, German, Italian, Japanese, Portuguese, Russian, and Spanish.

One of the major effects of national standards for the foreign language profession has been the expanded viewpoint of what makes up a comprehensive foreign language education. A quick glance at the five goal areas of the standards illustrates the point, as one quickly observes that language learning is not only a matter of learning how to communicate and learning about the cultures where different languages are spoken; this expanded view of a broad foreign language education also includes connecting with other disciplines to acquire information, developing insight into the nature of language and culture, and participating in multilingual communities at home and around the world.

While many good foreign language teachers have incorporated elements from the above three goals into their classrooms for years, the general perception has been that the REAL role of the foreign language classroom was to teach students how to communicate in a language other than English and to teach them how to operate within the chosen language's culture(s). The national standards have now emphatically stated that these additional areas—connections, comparisons, and communities—are also critical to a well-rounded foreign language experience for our students.

As a result, teachers are spending days in staff development and professional conference workshops delving into the richness of the implications of these three additional goal areas for the foreign language classroom. The *connections* goal is causing teachers to take a critical look at the enhanced language learning effect afforded the learner when discipline-specific content is linked with language use. Furthermore, teachers are becoming more aware of the increased learning potential when their students are able to "acquire information and recognize the distinctive viewpoints that are only available through the foreign language and its cultures" (National Standards...Project 1999, 56). A great number of foreign language educators seem to be particularly pleased with the inclusion of the *comparisons* goal in our national standards. Teachers have known for years that students demonstrate increased awareness of first language and first culture as a result of second language and second culture experiences. However, the overt attention to this fact in the standards elevates the importance of this phenomenon in the language learning experience. Finally, taking language outside the walls of the classroom and into the *communities* where it is used—both at home and abroad—is a welcome message to foreign language teachers. The addition of this goal to the standards provides teachers further support to seek as many ways as possible to create language learning opportunities that involve the community, both by involving students in community-based settings and by bringing heritage speakers from the community into the classroom. Such experiences also go a long way in lighting the fire toward life-long learning in students, another focus area of the new standards.

Even with what some would consider the "normal" goals of communication and cultures, our national standards have expanded the thinking of foreign language educators. Beyond the definition of what students should know and be able to do, the *communication* goal has set forth a new way to view the act of communicating. Rather than seeing language as behavior that is divided among the four skill areas of listening, speaking, reading, and writing, the national standards set forth a new paradigm called the communicative modes (Brecht and Walton), blending the aforementioned skill areas into natural combinations that form interpersonal, interpretive, and presentational messages. Clearly, this new liberating and rational paradigm is stimulating thought and discussion by language educators throughout the nation. And even the goal of *culture* has been given a new perspective as the standards developers set forth the "culture triangle." For decades, classroom teachers have focused on teaching their students about the products and practices of target cultures, but oftentimes the missing element in these lessons has been the "why?" — why do these products and practices exist? The national standards implore language educators to consider the importance of our students' knowing and understanding the perspectives from which cultural products and practices emerge, with the assurance that such knowledge liberates the language learner and becomes the "true catalyst for crosscultural understanding" (National Standards... Project 1999, 49).

Why has this writer chosen to focus so much attention on the new messages contained within the national standards, when this chapter's topic is assessment? The answer is two-fold. First, the new information found in the standards is having and will continue to have a massive impact on the way teachers think about instruction and the way they provide instruction to learners; and anything that affects the learning environment of the classroom must also have an effect on the way student learning is assessed. Second, this writer wants to use the standards scenario as an example of how much time and energy American foreign language educators are investing in re-thinking and re-inventing foreign language learning for the 21st century classroom. Even for a decade and a half prior to the advent of national standards, foreign language educators in this country were highly preoccupied with rethinking language learning, due to the proficiency movement, which was kicked off by the release in 1982 of the *ACTFL Provisional Proficiency Guidelines*. There is no way to quantify the number of staff development workshops, professional presentations and teacher workdays that have been dedicated to revamping foreign language curriculum to be more reflective of proficiency-oriented instruction since 1982. The arrival of national standards on the scene has only escalated the perceived need to devote precious time, energy and material and human resources to integrating these new thoughts and concepts into the foreign language classroom. And all this energy is good; it should be happening. But the downside to all this investment is that while our instructional environment has come to reflect new thoughts and new ideas about effective foreign language teaching and learning, the assessment environment has remained stuck, by and large, in a traditional framework still very much based on written tests in order to allow student knowledge to be easily and defensibly calculated.

These days, it is safe to say that a probable majority of foreign language teachers at least conceptually strive for a performance-based classroom setting. Clearly, some are better equipped and better able to make that happen than others. Nonetheless, the performance-based attitude prevails in this country as a means of addressing the need to produce "students who are equipped linguistically and culturally to communicate successfully in a pluralistic American society and abroad" (National Standards... Project 1999, 7). The only way the foreign language community — and the public that has been so supportive of this standards-based movement — will know the degree of success in reaching that goal is through assessment of student performance. Consequently, traditional measures (i.e., paper-and-pencil tests) do not afford students full opportunities to demonstrate all that they know and are able to do. Yet, such traditional measurements actually pre-dominate in the United States as a fair and easily reportable way of quantifying student progress. The bottom line is that no matter how much innovation is brought to the learning environment, if the assessment scenario is not consonant, favorable results that point to success in the new learning environment will not be demonstrated.

AN EIGHT-STEP ASSESSMENT PLAN

What can classroom teachers at all levels of foreign language instruction, from kindergarten through the university years, do to adequately and appropriately measure student progress toward meeting the language performance goals that the profession has so eloquently articulated? Unfortunately, there is no one easy answer or quick fix to that question. But this writer believes that the implementation of a multi-step plan can ensure that an assessment program can be put in place that will allow students to demonstrate to the fullest extent all that they know and are able to do. The following eight sequential steps comprise this plan:

Step One   Accept the belief that instruction and assessment should be mirror images of each other.

Step Two   Examine current instructional practice. What is it composed of? How varied is it?

Step Three	Contrast current assessment practice with current instructional practice. Are the two approached and manifested in the same way? If there are differences, what are they?
Step Four	Modify assessment practice, as necessary, making sure that performance-based assessment occupies a major place in the assessment plan.
Step Five	Use the ACTFL Performance Guidelines for K-12 Learners to frame expectations of how well students will perform language tasks.
Step Six	Consider the value of rubrics to measure student performance when global tasks are employed.
Step Seven	Determine those elements of the language learning experience that are most appropriately assessed by tests .
Step Eight	Consider the importance of student involvement in the assessment of their own progress and that of their peers.

Let's take a close look at each of these steps and examine their particular value in making this plan effective.

Step One   ***Accept the belief that instruction and assessment should be mirror images of each other.***

Clearly, every educator believes that students should be assessed on what they have been taught. But the required addition to that statement is that students should be assessed in the *ways* they were taught, so that instruction and assessment become mirror images of each other not only in content, but in *form,* as well. All of the professional development opportunities mentioned previously, in which teachers have participated over the past few years, have resulted in foreign language classrooms that look considerably different today from the way they looked twenty years ago. Partially the result of new national, state, and local standards and partially the result of a growing awareness of the public, in general, that Americans must be able to communicate in other languages to thrive in the 21st century, foreign language classrooms today are full of activities in which students gain functional ability in the language. Yet a close look at how students demonstrate *what they know and are able to do* often stops short, with simply demonstrating what they *know.* This scenario clearly does not allow instruction and assessment to mirror each other in form. Language educators must realize that if students learn how to use language in a variety of ways in the classroom, the only fair way to find out what they can do with the language is to have them demonstrate that use in a similar variety of ways.

For a portion of his career, this writer served as a high school assistant principal and during that time saw a long-held hunch validated. That hunch was that there was no classroom in the American high school that was more activity dominated than the foreign language classroom. While students in other disciplines were unfortunately often observed organized in long straight rows facing a chalk board (with many students appearing in a comatose state), foreign language students were engaged in a multitude of activities that involved movement around the room and, oftentimes to the consternation of more than one building principal, a great deal of noise. That same variety that is represented in the classroom learning setting must be mirrored in the assessment setting if we are to assess student knowledge and skills fairly.

Step Two   ***Examine current instructional practice. What is it composed of? How varied is it?***

Once teachers acknowledge the validity of the mirror image concept, the next step in this plan is to examine current instructional practice. Teachers should make a list of the kinds of activities they employ in class to help students learn how to use the language. No doubt this list will include a large variety of activities that take on many different forms. Some will be individual tasks, while others will involve pairs, triads or small groups. Some will be oral, and others will be written. Some will involve movement and consultation with classmates or community members, and others will involve use of reference materials in the classroom or the school media center. The commonality will be their variety. (See Chapter 3 for treatment of standards-based instruction.)

The learning scenarios that are included in the Standards provide rich insights into the variety of instructional activities that often exist in a standards-based classroom. Intended to serve as concrete examples of good practice, these scenarios show how the interweaving of the standards makes for a more cohesive and comprehensive experience for the learner. At the same time, these classroom instructional modules emphasize the variety of activities in which students participate in a standards-based classroom. The learning scenario given below, taken from the Spanish section of *Standards for Foreign Language Learning in the 21st Century* (467), can

can serve as an excellent example of good instructional practice that is full of a variety of learning avenues for students.

LOS ESTEREOTIPOS Y EL PREJUICIO

Students initiate this unit by discussing stereotypes found in their own communities, e.g., athletes, cheerleaders, blondes, redheads. The teacher leads a discussion that leads students to begin to realize that people are more alike than different, using a Venn diagram to categorize similarities and differences. Before beginning the question of stereotypes for Hispanic people, the teacher assesses attitudes, encouraging students to write about their feelings on issues of immigration, undocumented workers, and *maquiladoras*. A number of readings, chosen for the students' level of comprehension, lead them into a study of issues. Readings such as *La sandía*, by Anderson Imbert; *La mariposa* (Denevi); *Juan Darién* (Quiroga); works by Francisco Jiménez *(Capas de cartón, Mariposa)* illustrate the emotions of the issues in question. Spanish speakers visit the classroom and students interview them. Students also find information via the Internet. Several films, shown either in complete or edited versions, culminate the unit. Examples are *El norte*, The Ballad of Gregorio Cortez, My Family/*Mi familia*. Finally, students are asked to write again, in a journal, their thoughts and reflections of a possible change in attitude as a result of the unit. The teacher acts as a facilitator, without expressing opinions, in order to encourage students to form their own opinions. The teacher brings the unit to a close by focusing again on the problems of prejudice and stereotypes in the school and community.

The Standards then provide the following reflection or summary of the standards that are put into play through the above scenario:

1.1   Students discuss in Spanish a variety of stereotypes in their own society and interview native speakers on attitudes and emotions toward issues.

1.2   Students demonstrate an understanding of the issues, following readings and after viewing films.

1.3   Students role-play and present reports on materials they collect.

2.1   Students interpret cultural behaviors that might impede understanding of a culturally diverse population.

3.1   Students research issues in books and via the Internet.

4.1, 4.2 Students compare languages, translations, and sources of misunderstandings and make comparisons between Spanish and English.

5.1   Students find opportunities to employ Spanish to obtain further information.

5.2   Students complete the unit having attained a greater level of understanding of the source of cultural conflicts.

Examples such as this scenario provide perfect illustrations of the vast variety of instructional experiences encountered by foreign language learners in standards-based classroom settings.

Step Three   Contrast current assessment practice with current instructional practice. Are the two approached and manifested in the same way? If there are differences, what are they?

After listing classroom instructional activities, teachers should then make a list of the methods they use to assess what their students know and are able to do. As they make their lists, teachers should be aware that tests, even when there is variety in the kinds of tests given (vocabulary, unit, chapter, cumulative homework grades that count as a major test), are still tests and should be counted as only one way that students are assessed. Furthermore, consideration must be given to the ability of tests to measure what we want students to demonstrate. (Step 7 provides more insights on the value and limitations of tests.) After the teacher has completed making the assessment list of activities/methods, if there seems to be a much longer list of classroom instructional activities than assessment methods, the teacher should continue reading the following steps. If the two lists are similar, one can assume the existence of the mirror image and further reading of this chapter may not be necessary, although it might prove enlightening.

Step Four   Modify assessment practice, as necessary, making sure that performance-based assessment occupies a major place in the assessment plan.

If there appears to be a mismatch between the variety of instructional practice methods and assessment methods, this is a signal to the teacher that current assessment practices do not provide a full range of opportunities for students to demonstrate all that they know and are able to do. While tests provide educators clean, easily quantifiable ways to find out what students know, they come up short in their ability to show us if students know how to apply what they have learned. This writer does not advocate throwing out tests, precisely because they are efficient mechanisms to determine student knowledge. But to allow students to show us what they can do, the education community must look to something more comprehensive, something that allows students to demonstrate certain abilities.

Performance-based assessment tasks provide a perfect vehicle for students to show what they know how to do with the foreign language they are learning. *Challenge for a New Era: Nebraska K-12 Foreign Language Frameworks* (Nebraska Department of Education) illustrates the enduring value of this assessment alternative:

> Performance assessments are designed to provide students with a variety of tasks and situations in which they can demonstrate their understanding and apply their knowledge, skills, and thinking processes in a variety of contexts (Marzano, 1993). Performance assessments provide teachers and students with accurate feedback about their capabilities. While traditional, paper-and-pencil testing reduces a student's classroom life to a collection of scores or grades, performance-based assessments in the foreign language classroom measure students' abilities to communicate in the target language in real-world contexts using their knowledge of the target language and culture (142).

Such an approach allows for students to see an immediate connection between that which they have been practicing in class and tasks that they may be asked to perform in a real world where the target language is used exclusively for communication. This revelation accounts for increased motivation in students, who often fail to see connections between traditional "classroom" language and the real world.

It is probably safe to say that most foreign language students enter the classroom for the first time with the expectation that they are going to learn how to understand and speak this new language as well as get some information about its culture. Students maintain this perspective until teachers demonstrate in very clear ways that such will not be the case. Sadly, students often learn quickly that foreign language class is a place where language is studied and where they practice learning how to use the language in various authentic situations, only to face tests that reduce what they know and are able to do to what they can put down on paper. The use of performance-based assessment tasks allows teachers to send the clear message to students that their ability to show what they have learned how to do is at least as important as their ability to demonstrate their understanding of language structure on tests.

Once a teacher is convinced about the value and importance of including performance-based assessment tasks into the assessment cadre of techniques, where does the teacher go for examples? Most current foreign language textbook series include samples of performance-based assessments, although the majority of their assessments are paper-driven. Other examples can be found in recent publications such as *Proficiency-Oriented Language Instruction and Assessment: A Curriculum Handbook for Teachers* (Tedick), *Challenge for a New Era: Nebraska K-12 Foreign Language Frameworks* (Nebraska Department of Education), and *Assessment Tasks for French, German, and Spanish* (Indiana Department of Education). All of these contain excellent examples of performance-based assessment tasks tied to state-level foreign language curriculum frameworks in the respective states. While these examples provide teachers tremendous insights into good task design, teachers should be encouraged to create their own tasks that align with their particular program's performance goals for students in the various levels. As they become more convinced of the merits of performance-based assessment, school districts and consortia of districts are devoting time and energy to the development of assessment tasks that truly allow students to demonstrate what curriculum outcome statements say they should be able to do. Clayton County (GA) Public Schools, Fairfax County (VA) Public Schools and the Central Jersey World Languages Professional Development Project (headquartered at the Princeton [NJ] Regional Schools) are excellent examples of this effort. (For addresses, see the list at the close of this chapter.) The following is an example of a performance-based assessment task developed by foreign language educators in the Clayton County (GA) Public Schools:

Year/Level: Spanish, Level 1

*Performance Statements:**   *Introduce self*
                               Write simple words and phrases
                               Use appropriate greetings and leave-
                                   takings

Description of task to student:
                               You have just received the address of a

---

*Performance statements in this task are taken directly from the Clayton County Public Schools Foreign Language Curriculum Framework, Level One.

Spanish-speaking student who wants an American penpal. Write a postcard introducing yourself and asking your new penpal for information about himself/herself. As you write your postcard, greet your penpal and then write 3-5 complete sentences about yourself. Finally, ask a question of your penpal and write an appropriate closing (goodbye) for your postcard.

Approximate Time Needed: *15-20 minutes*

Scoring Criteria:

     3   **Exceeds Expectations**
- *1 appropriate greeting*
- *5 or more sentences, one of which must be a question*
- *1 appropriate closing*
- *misspelling does not affect meaning*

     2   **Meets Expectations**
- *1 appropriate greeting*
- *3 complete sentences*
- *1 question*
- *1 appropriate closing*
- *misspelling does not affect meaning*

     1   **Does Not Meet Expectations**
- *Inappropriate or no greeting*
  Or
- *Fewer than three complete sentences*
  Or
- *Inappropriate or no closing*
  Or
- *Consistent misspelling affects meaning*

Performance-based assessment tasks like the one illustrated above incorporate what many educators believe are essential characteristics of well-designed tasks. Such tasks

- are aligned with the goals and standards established for classroom instruction
- are authentic (real-life), meaningful and worthwhile
- motivate students by their real-life nature
- have clear instructions
- are level appropriate
- set forth clear scoring criteria
- incorporate a variety of skills and allow for different student responses

Use of performance-based tasks is at the heart and soul of a well conceived foreign language assessment program and allows teachers to go a long way in making the foreign language classroom one where instruction and assessment are mirror images of each other in content and form.

Step Five   *Use the ACTFL Performance Guidelines for K-12 Learners to frame expectations of how well students will perform language tasks.*

When the American Council on the Teaching of Foreign Languages, the American Association of Teachers of French, the American Association of Teachers of German, and the American Association of Teachers of Spanish and Portuguese were developing the foreign language standards, June Phillips (Weber State University), who served as the project director, was often heard explaining to audiences throughout the country that the job of the Standards Task Force was to define what students should know and be able to do, *not* how well they should know it or how well they should be able to do it. But clearly, the "how well" piece of the puzzle was an important one that needed to be added if a comprehensive picture of foreign language education was indeed to emerge. With a grant from the U.S. Department of Education, ACTFL subsequently received funding to answer the question "how well?" and the result appears in the form of the *ACTFL Performance Guidelines for K-12 Learners*, published in 1999. While foreign language educators have for years looked to the *ACTFL Proficiency Guidelines* (1986) for guidance about realistic performance, these guidelines were written to describe language performance in adults. Consequently, in the K-12 spectrum of instruction, they provided some assistance in determining how well high school learners could perform, since these students are characteristically more like adult learners; however, the Proficiency Guidelines were of little use in setting performance expectations for elementary and middle school students.

The *ACTFL Performance Guidelines for K-12 Learners* take into consideration the various enrollment configurations that exist in American schools and outline the kinds of language performance that can be expected for students, depending on the length and nature of their language learning experiences. A quick look at the guidelines reveals an organizational format that is familiar to most language educators. Descriptions are classified into three learner ranges: novice, intermediate, and pre-advanced. For example, a student who is in 10th grade and did not start his language learning until 9th grade would find descriptions of his performance in the Novice learner range. A 7th grade student who started language learning in kindergarten would find his appropriate performance descriptors in the Intermediate learner range. To provide the greatest amount of guidance to teachers in setting realistic expectation parameters for their students, each of the learner ranges is divided into six additional descriptive areas:

- **Comprehensibility** (How well is the student understood?)
- **Comprehension** (How well does the student understand?)
- **Language Control** (How accurate is the student's language?)
- **Vocabulary Use** (How extensive and applicable is the student's language?)
- **Communication Strategies** (How does the student maintain communication?)
- **Cultural Awareness** (How is the student's cultural understanding reflected in his language communication?)

While all of the descriptors given within the guidelines are based on information contained within the national standards, one obvious connection is the grouping of language performance descriptors into examples of interpersonal, interpretive, or presentational communication. The great value of these guidelines to a teacher who is transitioning to a performance-based assessment design is that they provide assistance in framing realistic student performance expectations, given the time they have been involved in language learning.

Step Six   *Consider the value of rubrics to measure student performance when global tasks are employed.*

Once performance-based assessment becomes a central part of an assessment plan, it is likely that students, teachers, parents, and administrators will all view such assessment measures as good and helpful preparation for future use of the language. However, the point of greatest concern will be how they are scored. Teachers first must be willing to accept that objective grading cannot be used in measuring performance and that there must be a move toward more subjective grading to account for a host of variables that are not present in discrete-point testing situations. In a previous section, this chapter has mentioned the fact that traditional scoring measures do not work well with performance-based assessment tasks. If there is any doubt about this statement, one might try grading a student skit using a traditional 100-point scale. Certainly, it can be done, but how easily is the teacher able to explain to students, parents and administrators why one skit received a 72 and why another skit received an 95? By their very design, performance-based assessment tasks might involve multiple skills and a variety of subtasks. Since they are more comprehensive in design—and in their execution—they beg for more global forms of scoring. To address this scoring dilemma, educators across disciplines are becoming increasingly comfortable with the use of rubrics to measure student performance in task-oriented assessments.

Rubrics tend to fall into two major categories: *holistic* and *analytic*. Holistic rubrics are used when the teacher wishes to score the student's language performance as a whole, with one grade. The use of such a rubric allows the teacher to provide an overall impression of the performance (Tedick). The performance task example described earlier (self-introduction through a postcard) uses a holistic rubric, which assigns one grade for the entire task.

Analytic rubrics are employed when the teacher wishes to place more attention on various pre-determined areas of focus. Such a rubric might focus on comprehensibility, language control, communication strategies, and pronunciation and look something like this:

Comprehensibility

   1   2   3   4   _____

Language Control

   1   2   3   4   _____

Communication Strategies

   1   2   3   4   _____

Pronunciation

   1   2   3   4   _____

                                                      Total   _____

As the reader can observe, this particular rubric will yield a score for the assessment task that will be a composite score; that is, a sub-score is assigned for the student's performance in each category and then all subscores are compiled to provide the total score.

Of course, teachers may use both types of rubrics in scoring a variety of tasks. The type of rubric chosen depends upon what the teacher wishes to assess and the detail with which s/he wishes to assess. The most important rule in designing any rubric is to keep it simple; students who are to be judged on the basis of the rubric's application must certainly be able to understand the rubric prior to its use. In fact, a growing number of language educators believe that not only should students know about rubrics prior to their use, the students themselves should assist in their development. Fairfax County (VA) Public Schools have involved their foreign language students not only in the creation of rubrics but also in being trained in how to use them. The idea is that if students have been through mock situations in applying the rubrics, they will understand them better and will have new insights into what makes up below-expected performance, expected performance, and performance that exceeds expectations. Parents and administrators must also be able to understand the rubrics that are used to determine a performance grade. Teachers must be willing to spend time with both of these audiences, in advance, to solicit their support and understanding for using rubrics to measure student work that is done in a non-traditional manner.

Step Seven   *Determine those elements of the language learning experience that are most appropriately assessed by tests.*

Paper-and-pencil tests have been briefly discussed elsewhere in this paper, primarily as an inadequate way to measure language performance. While that thought remains true, it is not the intent of this writer to discourage foreign language teachers from using tests to measure what students know. Clearly, if one wishes to find out what students know about language, a test can provide definitive and easily quantifiable and reportable feedback and in a format that appeals to the comfort level of many adults, both inside and outside the education community. However, that fact should not let us "off the hook." Bachman states that "when we design a language test, we hypothesize that the test taker's language ability will be engaged by the test tasks" (682). Teachers need to test Bachman's hypothesis every time they create a test. They need to be thoughtful test developers, carefully constructing tests that engage the learner's ability to think beyond regurgitation of facts and that elicit applications of as much of what s/he knows as possible.

Step Eight   *Consider the importance of student involvement in the assessment of their own progress and that of their peers.*

One can imagine that foreign language students in the Fairfax County (VA) Public Schools who have participated in rubric training and application are better and more motivated students as a result of the effort. This assumption underscores the valuable role that students can play in assessment of their own progress and that of their peers.   When students are involved in the assessment process, they understand better what the teacher is looking for and become more invested in the learning process as a whole.   In d'Anglejan, et. al., Nunan is even quoted as suggesting that "in a learner-centered system, students can be assisted to develop as autonomous learners by systematic use of self-assessment" (116). And when they become involved in assessing their peers (as through peer checklists on performance), they see better how their own performance might be improved. Grounlund, also quoted by d'Anglejan, observed that "judgment and reports made by students themselves are a valuable source of information in many areas of learning and development" (116).   It seems, then, that greater student involvement in the assessment arena can only yield favorable results for the foreign language classroom environment.

Students can become more involved players in assessment by the use of:

- Performance objective checklists (global or chapter-specific)

    I can . . . _____Ask or tell where something or someone is,
                          using directions
             _____Request and give an address
             _____Conduct a simple phone conversation

- Self-diagnosis of problem areas (e.g., problems in reading, listening)
- Evaluation activities (e.g., giving opinions about the effectiveness of various classroom activities; course evaluation; teacher evaluation)
- Reflections on learning (e.g., reflecting on what students have learned, what language they have used, where they have used the foreign language, what they feel they need to work on, how they would rate their progress).

Through these techniques and others, foreign language educators can make great strides in producing language students who become invested partners in the learning process.

CONCLUSION

The teaching of foreign languages in this country looks vastly different today from the way it looked twenty years ago. Armed with a growing body of research-based professional literature and experience, foreign language teachers are better prepared than ever to provide classroom experiences that lead students toward the ability to function in a second language. The advent of national, state and, in some cases, local standards and descriptions of realistic performance that can be expected from students after certain amounts of exposure to language learning has enabled teachers to teach with confidence and students to achieve unprecedented second language performance. However, without assessment mechanisms that measure what students have been learning and in the ways they have been learning, there is little likelihood that the foreign language community will be able to demonstrate the results of all its labors. How tragic a conclusion for all the heroic efforts that have been put forth to truly produce language-proficient students! Following the steps outlined in this chapter offers some possibilities of avoiding that lamentable paradox of having produced language users in the classroom who were rendered tongue-tied in the assessment venue because the assessment did not provide them the opportunity to show what they had learned how to do.

WORKS CITED

American Council on the Teaching of Foreign Languages. ACTFL Provisional Proficiency Guidelines. Yonkers, NY: ACTFL, 1982.

American Council on the Teaching of Foreign Languages. ACTFL Proficiency Guidelines. Yonkers, NY: ACTFL, 1986.

American Council on the Teaching of Foreign Languages. ACTFL Performance Guidelines for K-12 Learners. Yonkers, NY: ACTFL, 1999.

Bachman, Lyle F. "What Does Language Teaching Have to Offer?" TESOL Quarterly 25 (1991): 671-704.

Brecht, R.D., and A.R. Walton. "The Future Shape of Foreign Language Learning in the New World of Global Communication: Consequences in Higher Education and Beyond." Foreign Language Learning: The Journey of a Lifetime. Eds. Richard Donato and Robert M. Terry. Lincolnwood, IL: National Textbook Company, 1994. 110-152.

Clayton County Public Schools. Clayton County Schools Foreign Language Curriculum Framework, Level One. Morrow, GA, 1994.

d'Anglejan, Allison, et.al. "Student Evaluation in a Multidimensional Core French Curriculum," The Canadian Modern Language Review 49 (1990): 106-124.

Indiana Department of Education. Assessment Tasks in French, German and Spanish. Indianapolis, IN, 1993.

Marzano, R. J., et al. Assessing Student Outcomes: Performance Assessment Using the Dimensions of Learning Model. Aurora, CO: McREL Institute, 1993.

National Standards in Foreign Language Education Project. Standards for Foreign Language Learning: Preparing for the 21st Century. Lawrence, KS: Allen, 1996.

National Standards in Foreign Language Education Project. Standards for Foreign Language Learning in the 21st Century. Lawrence, KS: Allen, 1999.

Nebraska Department of Education. Nebraska K-12 Foreign Language Frameworks. Lincoln, NE, 1996.

Tedick, Diane J., ed. Proficiency-Oriented Language Instruction and Assessment: A Curriculum Handbook for Teachers. Minneapolis, MN: University of Minnesota, Center for Advanced Research in Language Acquisition: 1998.

CONTACT INFORMATION FOR PERFORMANCE-BASED TASKS

Central Jersey World Languages Professional Development Institute

Martin J. Smith, Director
Princeton High School
151 Moore Street
Princeton, NJ 08540
609-683-4480

Clayton County Public Schools

Joe Hairston, Superintendent
Judy Commander, Languages Arts Coordinator
2284 Old Rex Morrow Road
Morrow, GA 30260
404-362-3807

Fairfax County Public Schools

Martha Abbott, Foreign Language Coordinator
7423 Camp Alger Avenue
Falls Church, VA 22042
703-208-7722
E-mail: mabbott@fc.fcps.k12.va.us
Web site: http://www.fcps.k12.va.us/DIS/OHSICS/forlang/

Heritage Learners Of Spanish

Ana Roca
Florida International University

Historical Background

In the United States, where Spanish has traditionally been taught as a second or foreign language, the pedagogical issues of teaching Spanish to Spanish speaking students were historically largely ignored in our nation's schools and colleges. In the 1970s, the situation began to change slowly. Heated debates over bilingual education, the role of minority languages, and the growth of the Hispanic bilingual population in schools and colleges caused the Spanish teaching profession to examine its practices with regard to Spanish-speaking students in our Spanish language classes.

It was in the 1970s and 1980s when we saw the number of Spanish for native speaker courses increase. By 1993, however, only 22 percent of colleges and universities reported courses designated for native speakers of Spanish. Part of the problem may lie in the adequacy of informal surveys. Which colleges does one survey, and who sponsors the efforts? In the 1990s the American Association of Teachers of Spanish and Portuguese (AATSP) and other organizations looked into means of finding out more about curriculum and instruction for Spanish for Native Speakers (SNS) (Roca and Pino) in both secondary schools and colleges. In 1994, the *Chronicle of Higher Education* featured a front-page article about the legitimacy and the need for Spanish courses for heritage speakers (Collison). In addition, professional associations and other organizations have played important roles in bringing attention to the issues surrounding the needs of the Spanish-speaking students.

Heritage language instruction—similar to language arts, but not identical—has been growing at a steady pace just as the U.S. Hispanophone population has grown. The terminology used to describe this group of learners is particularly faddish: thus,

92 CHAPTER 5

"Spanish-speaking" or "Spanish S" students became "U.S. Hispanic bilingual" students or "home background" speakers, and are currently most commonly referred to as "heritage language" speakers. Whatever one wishes to call them, these are usually students who have grown up in Spanish-speaking or bilingual homes, but who have done most or all of their schooling in the dominant language, English. Because most of the formal education of these students has been in English and because the study of foreign languages is not a uniform or national requirement, these students have a wide range of academic training in the Spanish language as well as different levels of proficiency and literacy.

CONTINUED GROWTH OF U.S. LATINO STUDENT POPULATION IN SPANISH LANGUAGE COURSES

As was indicated above, the number of Hispanic bilingual university students studying Spanish in native speaker courses is unknown. We do know, however, that the number of these courses at all levels of the educational system has grown tremendously throughout much of the country. For example, the Miami-Dade County Public School system, the fourth largest in the nation, has over 93,000 students enrolled in K-12 Spanish for native speaker courses (1998-1999 school year). Miami-Dade Community College, the largest community college in the country, Broward Community College, the University of Miami, Florida International University, Florida Atlantic University, Broward County Public Schools, and many private schools in Miami offer substantial numbers of SNS classes at various levels of instruction. In other parts of the country, single SNS as well as two- or three-course tracks have been developed in secondary schools, community colleges and universities, to better meet the needs of the burgeoning Spanish-speaking student population. We also know that sometimes native speakers are placed in classes that are meant for beginning or intermediate non-native students of Spanish. While mixed classes are a reality in many schools and colleges, they do a disservice to heritage language students, who have different pedagogical and linguistic needs from those of the non-native speaker of Spanish. Particularly in the first two years of instruction, heritage language learners can benefit much more and progress much faster in separate tracks from the foreign language (FL) learner.

IN SEARCH OF APPROPRIATE PEDAGOGIES AND CURRICULUM

"Why isn't a curriculum designed to teach Spanish as a foreign or second language appropriate for heritage speakers?" Anyone who has been teaching Spanish long enough surely has heard this query from students, parents, administrators, even department heads. There are a number of reasons. Particularly problematic are the elementary and intermediate levels of instruction. While a second language learner is struggling to learn how to use basic oral greetings like *Hola, ¿qué tal? ¿Cómo andas?*, the heritage speaker can conduct chatty conversations, albeit with the use of non-standard forms and a discourse that may be marked by frequent code-switching (mixing of English and Spanish in an utterance). With varying degrees of proficiency, heritage speakers already comprehend and speak the language. Foreign language learners don't. Just as a first-level class in English for Speakers of Other Languages (ESOL) would be inappropriate for even the least accomplished and schooled native speaker of English, so are beginning FL classes wrong for native speakers of Spanish.

So what do these students need? Many of them use Spanish at home and with peers, but lack formal training in the language and have a limited bilingual range. As a result, their literacy skills in Spanish (most obviously, their non-standard spelling), their registers, vocabulary, and general ease and fluency with the language, need attention and expansion. These aspects, of necessity, also call students and teachers to examine their own sociolinguistic circumstances, their cultural heritage, and the phenomenon of bilingualism in a world that increasingly demands greater literacy and communicative abilities in professional and business spheres.

From the 1970s to the present, we also witnessed the publication of a number of scholarly articles on heritage Spanish speakers, with a focus on pedagogy and sociolinguistics, addressing such concerns as: 1) issues related to teaching the standard to learners who often use a stigmatized variant of Spanish, 2) how to address the problem of multiple cultures and literacy levels usually found in the same class, 3) the question of proficiency assessment and practical placement into a particular track or program in a school or college, 4) the need to select and create materials that address the linguistic and educational needs of specific groups of SNS students from different parts of the United States and Latin America, and 5) the need to develop new materials to help students a) expand their bilingual range and biliteracy, and b) better understand the phenomenon and the value attached to being a bilingual and bicultural individual who belongs to a linguistic minority in a given speech community.

THE AATSP: RESPONDING TO THE NEED FOR TEACHER TRAINING

Particularly in the last decade, the American Association of Teachers of Spanish and Portuguese (AATSP) has been reaching out to teachers and shifting its focus to the Spanish heritage language learner. Not only does the AATSP now have a standing national Committee on Teaching Spanish for Native Speakers, it has made a commitment to making a difference in this area by becoming more proactive, allocating time, energy, and budget to the improvement of SNS instruction on a national scale.

In the late nineties, AATSP director Dr. Lynn Sandstedt asked its SNS Committee to compile and write what would be the first volume in a professional development series handbook for teachers K-16, titled *Spanish for Native Speakers.* Dr. Sandstedt has often commented that the AATSP office frequently receives phone inquiries from teachers in need of assistance regarding SNS instruction and programs, seeking basic, accessible information on teaching these courses. The handbook serves as a practical guide and resource for new and experienced teachers and administrators, and it will also serve as a tool in special teacher-training workshops which the AATSP plans to offer in schools and colleges.

The fact that the AATSP saw fit to make the first volume of the series one that deals with teaching Spanish for Native Speakers clearly speaks to the growth and importance of the topic in the new millenium. Even more important is the fact that the heritage learner, whether of Spanish, Chinese, or Haitian-Creole, is also included now in the national foreign language standards (National Standards in Foreign Language Education Project 1999). In Spanish, because of the sheer size of the U.S. Latino student population and the political significance being afforded national standards, the projected impact of the *Standards for Learning Spanish* (431-74) on teacher training, curriculum, and materials develop-ment will be especially significant.

ACTFL SNS ACTIVITIES AND COLLABORATION
ON A HERITAGE LANGUAGE PROJECT

The American Council on the Teaching of Foreign Languages (ACTFL) now hosts a Spanish for Native Speakers (SNS) Special Interest Group (SIG), which in just a few years has become one of the largest SIGs of the largest foreign language teachers' association in the country. The SIG organizes three sessions on SNS instruction at the annual meeting in November. Here, both college and school teachers present their work and concerns, and most important, help disseminate research findings and exchange ideas to improve their own curriculum, instruction, and teacher training.

The ACTFL SIG reaches out to the broader Spanish teaching community as well. An SNS Internet discussion group has been set up. Teachers or administrators who would like to join a discussion can ask a question, contribute a book review, or comment on a teaching strategy or on an issue of curriculum development or school policy, and all can now access the SNS List easily. The idea, which originated at an ACTFL SNS meeting a few years ago, was carried out through the courtesy of one of the SIG members and Cornell University, which provides the server. (For more information on ACTFL and its annual conference, the SNS-SIG, or the SNS Internet List, see the ACTFL contact information in the Appendix to this volume.)

In the late nineties ACTFL went further and obtained a FIPSE grant (Fund for the Improvement of Post Secondary Education), together with Hunter College High School and Hunter College, involving the teaching of Spanish to native speakers and Haitian Creole. This professional development grass roots project, under the leadership of Dr. John Webb and Jamie Draper, involved a number of New York City public school teachers and administrators working with experts in the field and from ACTFL in the creation of a teacher training curriculum model via invitational colloquia, working meetings, readings, and work with heritage language teachers and curriculum planners of both Spanish and Haitian Creole. Their three-year work will culminate with the publication of a book on the project, which is meant to facilitate the duplication of the project at other sites around the country. Among the possible outcomes of the project will be a course in heritage language education that is projected as a requirement at Hunter College's program in modern language education, with the idea of proposing a similar requirement later on for state certification.

The National Foreign Language Center

The National Foreign Language Center (at Johns Hopkins University) is also at the forefront in heritage language research and education. The NFLC received a FIPSE grant in the late 1990s for a project involving heritage language speakers of the less commonly taught languages (such as Chinese, Arabic, and Korean). However, the center is also most interested in improving nationwide SNS instruction and teacher training. Currently the NFLC is working on a universally-available resource on SNS instruction and on more efficient ways to promote awareness and disseminate improvements in methodology and materials while working with all the appropriate professional organizations (like the AATSP and ACTFL) who also support professional development efforts in schools and higher education. One of the Center's projects is known as LangNet, a one-stop web resource in foreign languages for teachers and students. The Spanish Board of the project is working closely to develop a useful and rich resource of information on Spanish as a foreign language and as a heritage language. For more information on the NFLC and LangNet, as well as other projects involving heritage languages in the United States, visit their web site (see Appendix B).

THE CENTER FOR APPLIED LINGUISTICS

The Center for Applied Linguistics (CAL) has been at the forefront of the Heritage Language Initiative, which involved working collaboratively with the National Foreign Language Center, various professional associations, publishers, and the University of California at Long Beach, where Dr. María Carreira directs her university's Heritage Language Center with assistance from an NEH Challenge Grant. The collaborative initiative launched the first National Conference on Heritage Languages in the United States, held at Long Beach in October 1999, to be followed by a publication, with an agenda for action in public policy and education. CAL has also been compiling useful ERIC Digests (Pino; Lewelling and Peyton), MiniBibs, and a new type of publication, an Internet online resource guide, in the area of Spanish for Native Speakers (Roca and Marcos).

Additionally, with the University of California at Los Angeles (UCLA) and a grant from the National Endowment for the Humanities, CAL organized a Summer Institute for Teachers of Spanish for Native Speakers for summer 2000 at UCLA, with nationally recognized experts as faculty, to provide much needed training in this area to secondary school teachers who were selected from a national pool of applicants. A stipend was provided by NEH to cover such expenses as travel, housing, and books.

The persisting efforts for improvements on the part of the NFLC, the Center for Applied Linguistics, the AATSP, ACTFL, and other professional associations, as well as the efforts of individual dedicated teachers in our schools and colleges, are to be highly commended. With presentations, workshops, and summer institutes, the profession at large will be better prepared in the future to teach the heritage language learner.

THE RIGHT OF STUDENTS TO THEIR
OWN LANGUAGE—AND TO ITS DEVELOPMENT

In 1979, the Conference on College Composition and Communication, of the National Council of Teachers of English, affirmed "the right of students to their own language." At that time, the committee was referring to whatever variety of English students happen to speak. Mother tongue—in our case, Spanish—is also a student right that must be recognized in the United States. But beyond that right to the student's own language, the recent professional efforts to improve professional awareness, curriculum and instruction, and teacher training in heritage language education point toward the equally important right to maintain and develop one's mother tongue, to expand one's biliteracy in order to be better equipped for our world's demanding careers, professions and vocations. This newer path of constructive and positive thinking and of planning language-as-a-resource rather than language-as-a-problem, will help the United States review its capability and its goals regarding Spanish (and other languages) as useful natural reservoirs to be nourished and developed for practical uses in trade, international banking, and matters of foreign affairs.

THE NATIONAL STANDARDS

As part of the initiative of Goals 2000, the standards for foreign language learning were endorsed by 49 language organizations. The new standards, developed in the 1990s, recognize that successful language learning cannot have as its modus operandi simply the acquisition of the traditional skills of listening, speaking, reading, and writing. The standards provide a wider scope of the aspects involved in becoming proficient and literate in a language. In addition to the four skills, learning a language must also encompass interpreting and using appropriate registers, learning other elements of pragmatics, using strategies like circumlocution to keep communication from breaking down, judging one's audience, and improving one's presentational abilities in the language. Learning another language should be centered around learning about other cultures and reflecting upon one's own, learning about a variety of social issues and how to function in a variety of social contexts, interacting with the speakers of the language, and learning about their history, their literary heritage, and their popular culture across disciplines.

The new national standards take into account the reality of our diverse student population, where heritage language learners are present in mixed or separate classes. The organizing principles of language education, as provided by the standards, consist of the five Cs (communication, cultures, connections, comparisons, and communities), as have been already discussed at length elsewhere in other chapters of this volume. Where the Spanish heritage learner is concerned, the new standards allow for ample flexibility for teachers and students in terms of the development of classroom activities that focus on such aspects of instruction as: varied and rich cultural content, practicing useful learning strategies, learning content from other disciplines or subjects, developing critical thinking skills in Spanish, and using video and web technologies. The Spanish-specific standards (National Standards...Project 1999, 431-74) provide many further examples of classroom activities and projects that are appropriate for heritage learners of Spanish.

The national standards prescribe neither course content nor a curriculum *per se*. They do, however, provide a framework from which to work, and they indicate to us the types of learning experiences that can be most helpful to the widest range of Spanish language students. In years to come, the Spanish teaching profession will continue to construct learning tasks and design class activities and experiences that can help create a rich learning environment for the native speaker studying Spanish in school. Clearly, the standards have provided teachers with a new way of being informed about language learning and teaching, and in our case, a much more appropriate way of thinking about teaching Spanish as a heritage language.

The five goals of foreign language education, as outlined in the standards, are equally useful and important to FL and heritage Spanish students. How can Latino students profit from instruction based on the standards? To answer this question, we may examine each of the five goal areas.

Communicative Skills: Interpersonal, Interpretive, and Presentational Modes

When individuals have developed communicative competence in a language, they are able to convey and receive messages of many different types successfully. These individuals use language to participate in everyday social interactions and to establish relationships with others. They converse, argue, request, convince, and explain effectively, taking into account the age, background, education, and familiarity of the individuals with whom they are engaged in conversation.

National Standards...Project 1999, 40

In the United States, even if heritage language learners took some Spanish while in school, the bulk of their education and development of academic skills, both orally and in writing, has been in English. The standards' framework of communicative modes—the interpersonal, the interpretive, and the presentational—allows us to be flexible, creative, and practical where heritage learners are concerned. Many kinds of activities can be developed for the heritage speaker, once we know where they need the most assistance.

In the area of *communicative competence*, most heritage language learners can already interact in Spanish in and outside the classroom at varying levels of fluency. They can "participate in everyday social interactions and...establish relationships with others" (40). But their interpersonal skills are often better developed than their interpretive skills and their formal presentational skills, because they have typically used Spanish at home and in informal private and public settings, and they may have difficulty when communication must move beyond the realm of family and friends and into more formal domains. They must acquire experience using the language through face to face and written contacts that require a degree of formality they are unaccustomed to. This naturally leads to an examination of cultural differences, not only between U.S. social customs and those of Hispanics, but also among different Hispanic nationalities. A Spaniard's manner of expressing him or herself in a business communiqué can sound positively 19th century to the let's-not-beat-around-the-bush American. And yet being fully bilingual in a global marketplace might require that our U.S. Hispanic one day be able not only to understand but to reproduce that style of writing.

There are many other formal communicative contexts with which SNS students have had little experience. For example, few students have been exposed to listening to lectures or presentations in Spanish. Areas with large bilingual populations afford multiple and varied community events that students can attend for class credit. This can be an invaluable resource when we consider the interpretive domain of the communication component of the new standards, but it is also directly related to the presentational domain. How better to learn about making presentations than by regularly attending them?

Communities: Using the Language Away from Home and School

The areas focused on in the new standards are, by their very nature, inextricably linked; a visual representation of them looks not unlike the rings on the Olympic flag. Activities that promote communication may be naturally tied to community, for example, or to learning about culture and comparing what one has learned to one's own experience, thus making meaningful connections. In the best of worlds, all five curricular C's come together in the following activity: Students choose an interview subject from the community, develop topics to cover and questions, and conduct a formal interview in Spanish. They are encouraged not just to stick to their pre-formulated list of questions, but to allow their subjects to digress, to probe topics and sidelines which may come up in the course of their conversation. They must tape the interview and write an article about their interview subject which should demonstrate their awareness of other ways of communicating aside from just the spoken word, including gesture, eye contact, use of pauses, etc. They must then give an oral presentation in class, not just about the person, but also including their reflections on the interview process itself.

Connecting Across Disciplines, Across Cultures

The World Wide Web presents language students with a seemingly endless array of opportunities to connect easily with others, even across great distances, as well as to become connected to myriad sources of information. With so many options available, what do you pick? One activity that plugs students into the world of possibilities offered by the Web in terms of print journalism is following a controversial international news story. Different groups can be assigned the same item but different countries, or even different newspapers within one country. In addition to print media, radio broadcasts are increasingly available, introducing students to a wide range of accents and lexicons, as well as world views. This speaks directly to Standard 3.2 of the Spanish standards: "Students acquire information and recognize the distinctive viewpoints that are available only through the Spanish language and its many cultures." The point of reference for these students is always the coverage the story receives in one's hometown press, and they should be asked to compare what are often two very different takes on the same event.

Another way of using technology to make connections across other disciplines is planning an itinerary for a trip. Student groups are given a budget and a destination in the Spanish-speaking world. They must choose what to see, where to stay, and what to eat, and in so doing they must also demonstrate an awareness of and sensitivity for the different cultural practices in their destination country. This activity works best if students then have to present their itinerary to the class, and thus it also addresses Standard 1.3: "Students present information, concepts, and ideas to an audience of listeners or readers on a variety of topics." If they are really ambitious, you may want them to do this in the form of a PowerPoint presentation. The groups learn from one another about the historical places of interest in their destination country, local customs, the food, the exchange rate, the weather. (As an added bonus, I have had a number of students vow that they were really going to take the trips they had planned for their project.)

COMBINING THE STANDARDS AS A FRAMEWORK: A SAMPLE ACTIVITY FOR INTERMEDIATE TO ADVANCED SNS CLASSES

When I am teaching a unit on human rights, focusing on Latin America, based on the readings and topics found in *Nuevos mundos* (Roca 1999), my students become immersed in the topic in a number of ways which include the five frameworks of the standards. For example, after students have already read the book's introductory essay on human rights in Latin America, and discussed in class various related literary texts including poetry and short stories, I have students work on a number of activities in small groups or on their own. Each student, with partners or on their own, must see a film related to the unit topic. A list is provided at the end of the unit and the list is updated on the board on a regular basis. Most of the films are available in our university library, but I also recommend two or three local video stores that are well stocked in Spanish language films, and I let them know about video resources available for free (except for the cost of mailing—as through the *Instituto Cervantes*, the AATSP, and the OAS). I encourage them to view either feature films or good quality documentaries or educational videos.

One movie that I have often recommended is *La historia oficial*, which won an Oscar for best foreign film when it came out in the 1980s. I have them watch the film after they have seen in class an excellent documentary titled *Las madres de la Plaza de Mayo*, which better prepares them to understand the feature film in its historical context of the *guerra sucia* in Argentina. By reading on the topic, listening to the teacher's introduction to the topic of human rights violations in Latin America, in particular in the *Cono Sur* region, watching the documentary in class, and commenting about it afterward, students usually are more curious and better prepared to delve into the subject independently.

I explain to students that I want them to watch a film in the way that a film critic would watch it. This means that they need to seek out film reviews in Spanish to help them not just with style, but with vocabulary. I ask them to pretend that they are writing a review for their student newspaper and that they need to be as informative as possible but limit themselves to two to three type-written pages. I ask them to write a draft and revise it, to review it carefully before handing it in, and to read it aloud to hear how it sounds and how it flows. What if they had to read their review on the air for a radio show or for a TV spot?, I ask, emphasizing the importance of revision, conciseness, organization, and effective language. We discuss some of the main things that should be considered when writing a review, and we go over them on the board. For many of them, words like *la trama, el guión, el cineasta, el personaje principal*, etc., are new. We discuss the need to be informative and to interpret many aspects of a film, the need to be analytical as well as evaluative in writing the review.

I find that this assignment is very useful and motivating for students because it includes meaningful **communication** with their classmates. Students must first engage in understanding and interpreting what they watch. Later they must be able to write a film review and make an informed and convincing oral presentation about the film to the class. Watching the video, reading about similar themes, and at times doing some brief research on the web as a homework assignment also incorporate other standards. They will be studying about Argentinean culture in a given historical context, and they will make **connections** with other disciplines (Latin American studies, history, political science, international studies, economics, etc.) and they will make **comparisons** of the culture of Argentina of that time with their own in the United States. The idea that over 30,000 persons "disappeared" is shocking to anyone, and so much more to college students who were unaware of the many *guerras sucias* that have taken place in Latin America and elsewhere in the world. Finally, students come to see themselves not just connected as U.S. Latino students, but also as part of the larger Latin American **community**, becoming interested in current news about Latin America (via the Internet and cable television); they read updates on the human rights situation of other countries like Chile, Guatemala, El Salvador, Peru, Colombia, Honduras, Mexico, etc.

SNS students make further connections, realizing they are responsible for their own life-long learning in Spanish and that they can do this by applying the language for useful purposes: to be better informed as citizens, to be enriched with it for personal enjoyment, and to have better option to information through knowing another language and how to manipulate its information resources. In the end, asking students to gather information in Spanish from the web, for example, helps to give them a sense of greater empowerment, since they have an edge over monolingual seekers of information. The use of the standards in the Spanish for native speakers class will help teachers loosen the shackles of more rigid language teaching methodologies, reflecting different thinking on how languages are best learned and maintained.

Both learners and teachers will be freer to concentrate on content, ideas, meaningful and interesting class discussions, formal oral presentations based on library and on-line research on specific topics of interest, and such. Grammar and spelling will not be thrown out the window, but they will certainly take a seat on the sidelines for the moment. Eventually, for those who continue studying Spanish, these will fall into place, given more reading and exposure to the language. That exposure will be richer and more meaningful and engaging for the students as the intertwining elements represented by the five C's of the standards help us as guidelines in charting the directions our classes will take. In the coming years, with the leadership of teachers and the national organizations, and the textbook companies that will be steered towards publishing materials that cater to our changing needs in the classroom, new texts and activities will be created that reflect the standards as they specifically apply to Spanish heritage learners. We will be better teachers for the change, and our students will be better thinkers and communicators.

WORKS CITED

AATSP SNS Committee. *Spanish for Native Speakers*. Volume 1 of the AATSP Professional Development Series Handbooks for Teachers K-16. Fort Worth: Harcourt College Publishers, 2000.

Collison, Michele N.K. "Spanish for Native Speakers." *Chronicle of Higher Education* 40, 22 (February 1, 1994): 15-16.

Colombi, M.C., and F. X. Alarcón. *La enseñanza de español a hispanohablantes: praxis y teoría*. Boston: Houghton Mifflin, 1997.

Conference on College Composition and Communication. "Students' Right to Their Own Language." April 1974. http://www.ncte.org/ccc/12/

Lewelling, Vickie W., and Joy Kreeft Peyton. "Spanish for Native Speakers: Developing Dual Language Proficiency." *ERIC Digest*. Washington, D.C.: Center for Applied Linguistics, May 1999.

National Standards in Foreign Language Education Project. *Standards for Foreign Language Learning: Preparing for the 21st Century*. Lawrence, KS: Allen, 1996.

National Standards in Foreign Language Education Project. *Standards for Foreign Language Learning in the 21st Century*. Lawrence, KS: Allen, 1999.

Pino, Cecilia. "Teaching Spanish to Native Speakers: A New Perspective in the 1990s." *ERIC Digest*. Washington, D.C.: Center for Applied Linguistics, September 1997.

Roca, Ana. "Retrospectives, Advances, and Current Needs in the Teaching of Spanish to United States Hispanic Bilingual Students." *ADFL Bulletin* 29.1(1997): 37-44.

Roca, Ana, and Kathleen Marcos. "Resources for Teaching Spanish to Spanish Speakers." ERIC/CLL Resource Guides Online. ERIC Clearinghouse on Languages and Linguistics. November 1999. http://www.cal.org/ericcll/faqs/rgos/sns.htm

Roca, Ana, and Cecilia Pino. Unpublished survey, 1996.

Sandstedt, Lynn. Informal personal communication about the need for teacher training and basic information on teaching Spanish to native speakers. Spring 1999.

APPENDIX A

SELECTED RESOURCE LIST OF COLLEGE-LEVEL TEXTBOOKS FOR TEACHING SPANISH TO NATIVE SPEAKERS

Alonso-Lyrintzis, D., B. Zaslow, and H. Villareal. *Entre mundos*. New Jersey: Prentice-Hall, 1996.

Blanco, George, Victoria Contreras, and Judith Márquez. *¡Ahora sí!* Boston: Heinle & Heinle, 1995.

Burunat, Silvia, and Elizabeth Starcevic. *El español y su estructura: Lectura y escritura para bilingües*. New York: Holt, Rinehart, Winston, 1983.

De la Portilla, Marta, and Beatriz Varela. *Mejora tu español. Lectura y redacción para bilingües*. New York: Regents, 1979.

Elliott, Raymond A. *Nuevos Destinos: Español para hispanohablantes*. To accompany the Nuevos Destinos video series and optional CD-ROM. San Francisco: McGraw-Hill College, 1999.

Lequerica de la Vega, Sara, and Carmen Salazar Parr. *Avanzando. Gramática española y lectura*. [*Cuaderno B.*] New York: John Wiley & Sons, 1997.

Marqués, Sarah. *La lengua que heredamos: Curso de español para bilingües.* New York: John Wiley & Sons, 1986, 1992, 1996.

Mejías, Hugo A., and Gloria Garza-Swan. *Nuestro español: Curso para estudiantes bilingües.* New York: Macmillan Publishing Co., 1981.

Miguélez, Armando, and María Sandoval. *Jauja. Método integral de español para bilingües.* Englewood Cliffs, NJ: Prentice Hall, 1987.

Roca, Ana. *Nuevos Mundos: Lectura, cultura y comunicación.* New York: John Wiley & Sons, 1999. (With contributions by Helena Alonso and Eloy Merino.)

Samaniego, Fabián, Francisco X. Alarcón, and Nelson Rojas. *Mundo 21.* Lexingrton, MA: D.C. Heath, 1995.

Valdés, Guadalupe, and Richard V. Teschner. *Español escrito. Curso para hispanohablantes bilingües.* Cuarta edición. Englewood Cliffs, NJ: Prentice Hall, 1999.

APPENDIX B

TEACHING SPANISH AS A HERITAGE LANGUAGE: SELECTED ADDITIONAL READINGS

Aparicio, Frances R. "Diversification and Pan-Latinity: Projections for the Teaching of Spanish to Bilinguals." *Spanish in the United States: Linguistic Contact and Diversity.* Eds. Ana Roca and John M. Lipski. Berlin: Mouton, 1991. 183-198.

_____. "La enseñanza del español para hispanohablantes y la pedagogía multicultural." *La enseñanza del español a hispanohablantes: Praxis y teoría.* Eds. M. Cecilia Colombi and Francisco X. Alarcón. Boston: Houghton Mifflin, 1997. 222-32.

Benjamin, Rebecca. "What Do Our Students Want? Some Reflections on Teaching Spanish as an Academic Subject to Bilingual Students." *ADFL Bulletin* 29.1 (Fall 1997): 44-47.

Colombi, M. Cecilia, and Francisco X. Alarcón, eds. *La enseñanza del español a hispanohablantes: Praxis y teoría.* Boston: Houghton Mifflin, 1997.

Gutiérrez, John R. "Teaching Spanish as a Heritage Language: A Case for Language Awareness." *ADFL Bulletin* 29.1 (Fall 1997): 33-36.

Hidalgo, Margarita. "On the question of 'Standard' vs. 'Dialect': Implications for Teaching Hispanic College Students." *Hispanic Journal of Behavioral Sciences* 9 (1987): 375-95.

Merino, Barbara J., Henry T. Trueba, and Fabián Samaniego, eds. *Language and Culture in Learning: Teaching Spanish to Native Speakers of Spanish.* Washington, D.C. and London: The Falmer Press/Taylor & Francis, 1993.

Roca, Ana. "Retrospectives, Advances, and Current Needs in the Teaching of Spanish to United States Hispanic Bilingual Students." *ADFL Bulletin* 29.1 (Fall 1997): 37-44.

_____. "Teaching Spanish to the Hispanic Bilingual College Student in Miami." *Spanish in the United States: Sociolinguistic Issues.* Ed. J.J. Bergen. Washington, D.C.: Georgetown University Press, 1990. 127-136.

Valdés, Guadalupe. "Bilinguals and Bilingualism." *International Journal of the Sociology of Language* (IJSL) 172 (1997): 25-52.

_____. "Teaching Spanish to Hispanic Bilinguals: A Look at Oral Proficiency Testing and the Proficiency Movement." *Hispania* 73 (1989): 392-401.

_____. "The Teaching of Minority Languages as Academic Subjects: Pedagogical and Theoretical Challenges." *The Modern Language Journal* 79.3 (Fall 1995): 299-328.

_____. "The Teaching of Spanish to Bilingual Spanish Students: Outstanding Issues and Unanswered Questions." Colombi and Alarcón. 8-24.

Valdés, Guadalupe, Anthony G. Lozano, and Rodolfo García-Moya, eds. *Teaching Spanish to the Hispanic Bilingual in the United States: Issues, Aims, and Methods.* New York: Teachers College Press, 1981.

Valdés-Fallis, Guadalupe. "A Comprehensive Approach to the Teaching of Spanish to Bilingual Spanish-speaking Students." *The Modern Language Journal* 43.3 (1978): 101-110.

USING TECHNOLOGY
TO ADDRESS THE SPANISH STANDARDS

Jean W. LeLoup
SUNY Cortland

This chapter will discuss the role of technology in foreign language instruction and, in particular, its role in addressing the *Standards for Learning Spanish* (hereafter referred to as the Spanish Standards)(National Standards in Foreign Language Education Project 1999, 431-74). The chapter will explore 1) a definition of technology, 2) the national mandate for technology implementation across the curriculum, 3) how technology has been used heretofore in foreign language classrooms, and 4) how it can continue to aid educators in their quest to align their curricula with the Spanish Standards. A rationale for using technology in language instruction and learning will be offered that discusses some theoretical underpinnings and briefly touches on the research base for its implementation in the foreign language curriculum. Finally, the chapter will include some examples of the use of technology pertaining to particular learning Standards and sample Progress Indicators.

WHAT IS TECHNOLOGY?

The following statements, taken from the New Jersey Core Curriculum Content Standards,[1] seem to encompass much of what teachers perceive as the definition of technology:

- Technology may be defined as the process by which human beings fashion tools and machines to *change, manipulate,* and control their environment.
- Technology is the technical means people use to *improve* their surroundings.

- Technology is the knowledge of using tools and machines to do tasks *efficiently*.
- Technology is people using knowledge, tools, and systems to make their lives *easier* and *better*. (Brzezowski; italics added)

Often, the word "technology" strikes fear in the hearts of educators. They tend to think only in terms of the most modern technological advances, accompanied by steep learning curves, and frequently forget that they have, indeed, been using many forms of technology for years. Several examples of technology with which teachers are most likely familiar are: tape recorders, overhead and opaque projectors, the language lab, the VCR and videos, slide carousels, film strip projectors, laminators, photocopiers, even the 16 mm movie projector. These are all forms of technology that teachers use regularly to manipulate and change the learning environment, to make teaching more efficient, easier, and better, and to improve learning. At present we need to include newer technologies such as laserdiscs, computers, CDs, DVDs, LCD projection, flatbed scanners, digital cameras, distance learning, and the World Wide Web (WWW). Though not exhaustive, this list is fairly inclusive, and many of these technologies—old *and* new—are used on a regular basis in the foreign language (FL) classroom.

NATIONAL IMPETUS FOR TECHNOLOGY AND STANDARDS

The International Society for Technology in Education (ISTE) sponsors a project called National Educational Technology Standards (NETS), wherein an initial set of Technology Foundation Standards for Students in pre-kindergarten through 12th grade has been developed. This is the first step in a multiyear project aimed at describing the conditions needed to support the use of technology for learning, teaching, and institutional management across the curriculum. Standards under development and refinement include:

- Standards for using technology in learning and teaching—How technology should be used throughout the curriculum.
- Educational technology support standards—Systems, access, staff development, and support services essential to support the effective use of technology.

- Standards for student assessment and evaluation of technology use — Various means of assessing student progress and evaluating the use of technology in learning and teaching. (ISTE homepage 1999)

The NETS Project has developed six broad categories of technology foundation standards for students, with requisite skills to be mastered within each category:

- Basic operations and concepts
- Social, ethical, and human issues
- Technology productivity tools
- Technology communications tools
- Technology research tools
- Technology problem-solving and decision-making tools

The categories are meant to be introduced, reinforced, and mastered by students, and they provide a framework for linking to curriculum standards in specific content areas as well. (ISTE 2000). The NETS project provides performance indicators, activities, tools and resources, and content standards that directly correspond to particular subject area standards.[2]

In concert with the NETS project, the *Standards for Foreign Language Learning* (National Standards…Project 1999) includes technology as one of the principal elements in the "curricular weave" of language learning and instruction (33). The importance of technology continues to hold in addressing the Spanish Standards, as it can be used in a variety of ways to facilitate the "5 C" goal areas of Communication, Culture, Comparisons, Connections, and Communities.

WHY USE TECHNOLOGY?

Some very basic and important reasons for the many uses of technology on a regular basis in the foreign language classroom are: ease, convenience, availability, interest, and efficiency. Below are several ways in which teachers use technology for producing, preserving, and using instructional materials:

- Lamination of realia very carefully brought back from a target language country so that it would last.
- Photocopies of menus from McDonald's so that each student has an example to use in a class activity.

- The use of transparencies prepared ahead so that precious class time is not wasted writing all that information out on the spot.
- The use of an audio tape that allows a student to make up a listening portion of an exam or enables the teacher to create a new learning center in the classroom; both situations free the teacher for other activities.
- Repeatability of a lecture or lesson when captured on videotape so students can see it whenever necessary (Ervin).
- Delivery of FL classes via distance learning that otherwise would not be offered (Pitkoff & Roosen).
- Creation of instructional materials using presentational software such as PowerPoint, which is designed to get ideas across in an attractive, pleasing, and attention-getting manner.
- Supplementary computer materials available to those students who need an extra challenge or additional drill and practice and can work on their own at their individual pace.
- Availability of materials via technology: it is pervasive as textbook publishers these days rush to provide all kinds of technological ancillaries that will make their product competitive with the next one.
- Creation of tests, quizzes, and other worksheets that is much easier on a computer, particularly if you make a typing error.

These are just some general examples of how technology can benefit instruction. Clearly, teachers have all been using quite a bit of technology for years with satisfactory results. Now they have the opportunity to expand and incorporate new technologies into the curriculum in order to better address the standards, enhance instruction, and improve student learning. First, however, some theoretical issues need to be explored.

THEORETICAL ISSUES AND RESEARCH BASE

In 1991, in her seminal article entitled "Technology in the Service of Foreign Language Learning: Trends and Issues," Nina Garrett asked some pointed questions about the role of technology and its relationship to theory and practice in language instruction and learning:

1. Should the technology be thought of as primarily assisting teaching or as directly supporting learning?

2. What is the relationship between a theoretically and empirically based understanding of the language learning process and the design and implementation of technology-based materials?

3. Should students work with pedagogically shaped materials or directly with authentic data?

4. Should student access to the material be directed or entirely under their own control?

5. What kinds of research does the use of technology for language learning demand or enable?

(Garrett, "Technology" 74)

Again in 1993, Gerard Ervin revisited the issue with similar questions as he grappled with the overarching query "Can Technology Fulfill its Promise?"

1. Are we making the right demands on technology?
2. Are we asking the right questions about technology?
3. Are we prepared to interact effectively with technology? (7)

In "A Communications Technology Module for the Foreign Language Methods Course," LeLoup devoted one section precisely to many of these same concerns; that is, underscoring issues to consider in planning to use communications technologies in the language classroom:

1. What are my objectives for the lesson?
2. What do I expect the students to be able to accomplish or do at the end of the lesson?
3. Will any of these communications technologies facilitate the students' success in achieving the lesson objectives?
4. Which, if any, communications technologies are best suited to the particular tasks I have chosen for my students to perform?
5. Will the use of technology hinder or help the students; i.e., are they adequately and appropriately trained in the use of the technologies?
6. Do I feel competent in using the communications technologies I am asking my students to use?
7. Am I just using these bells and whistles because it's Friday and/or I didn't plan adequately for my lesson?

These questions should be the very foundation of our choice to use technology to achieve better instruction. In other words, is the decision to use technology a principled one? Are there theoretical underpinnings for the implementation of technology in the foreign language classroom?

Frequently, the question arises: "Where is the research base that justifies all the use of technology?" This is an excellent question, and one we can ill-afford to ignore in our profession. The field of Second Language Acquisition (SLA) is a relatively young discipline, dating from the late 60s with the seminal article by S. Pitt Corder on learner errors and Larry Selinker's 1972 article on Interlanguage. Since those years, we have sifted and shifted through various methodologies and approaches and have finally settled, for the time being, anyway, on the communicative approach to language instruction. In the foreign language profession, we have a reputation for trying one new idea or fad method after another in our eternal search for *the* way to teach and learn second languages. Very often we have made these switches without any more guidance than "gut reaction" or intuition. Sometimes those guides are accurate, but they are not, of themselves, a sufficient basis for determining the direction of an entire field of study. We need an empirical database of evidence that underscores what does, in effect, constitute productive language instruction and learning.

Unfortunately, we are hampered by a veritable plethora of SLA theories, many of which are intuitively appealing but most of which are either not testable in large part or leave some portions of acquisition unexplained or even unaddressed. On top of this, now we also need to show that integrating technology into the curriculum is a worthwhile exercise, both for teachers and learners. In reality, the empirical database that would supply the evidence necessary is truly fledgling. At this time, there simply are not many articles detailing studies that aim to establish the effectiveness of technology for language learning and instruction. Controlling the myriad variables involved is an overwhelming challenge, and because we are still quite hard-pressed to prove precisely what <u>does</u> cause language learning, it is rather difficult to design a study that shows that the use of technology enhances the "whatever" that activates learning.

THEORETICAL FRAMEWORK OR UNDERPINNINGS

Given the above circumstances and difficulties, several researchers advocate establishing a theoretical framework for the inclusion of technology in second language instruction (Garrett, "Language Pedagogy" and "Technology"; Ervin; Salaberry ; Zhao). This principled approach is the only feasible one, lest we once again jump on another bandwagon only to fall off later. Nowadays, there is much proliferation of technology monies, and schools are scrambling again to install new computer learning centers complete with all the latest technologies available. This is great, but utilization of technology for technology's sake is not a sound basis for instruction. We can use technology efficiently and effectively, but not without beginning from some pedagogically sound principles that reflect theoretical underpinnings.

Below are some basic premises, generally accepted in the language acquisition field (Zhao), that lead us toward a principled approach to the integration of technology in language instruction:

1. Language learners must have meaningful second language input. In other words, they must be exposed to second language input that is comprehensible to them and delivered in context (Ellis, *Understanding* and *The Study*; McLaughlin).

2. Language learners need to interact with the target language. They need to engage in meaningful activities that have them manipulate the second language and negotiate meaning (Doughty and Pica; Long).

3. Learning the culture of the target language is an integral part of learning the second language (Lambert et al.; Seelye; Seliger).

4. Motivation, although not completely understood, is nevertheless an important factor in second language learning (Gardner; Gardner and Lambert).

5. Language learners need exposure to authentic materials in order to be able to function in a target language environment (Ellis, *Understanding*).

How and where does technology fit into the above tenets of SLA theory and research? More specifically, how can we implement new technologies in a principled manner to address the Spanish Standards and effect positive learning outcomes?

THE ROLE OF TECHNOLOGY IN IMPLEMENTING THE SPANISH STANDARDS

One of the biggest advantages to using modern technologies in the classroom is the access they afford to real Spanish language input from authentic materials. Teachers in rural or isolated areas, teachers who are the only foreign language teacher in their schools ("singletons"), and those who for whatever reasons cannot travel to Spanish-speaking countries with any frequency are particularly disadvantaged in that they are hard-pressed to come up with the authentic materials and native language input that are so important to second language classrooms. With the advent of many new communications technologies, this access is now much more readily available. The Internet has opened many doors to us as Spanish teachers. We can read Spanish language newspapers on-line daily. We can listen to foreign news broadcasts and even see them through the technologies of streaming audio and video. We can engage in synchronous and asynchronous conversations with native speakers on a regular basis—and so can our students.

The ancillary materials currently available on CD-ROM and the particular Internet sites that coordinate with Spanish textbooks are rife with authentic materials, native speaker input, and a cultural richness that were absent for so long from traditional texts and workbook versions. These materials contain digitized audio and video segments that expose the language learner to real-life situations, contextualized language instruction, and embedded cultural information that clearly enhance the language learning experience.

Access to authentic materials and native speaker input is a powerful argument in favor of the implementation of technology in the curriculum. Indeed, it is underscored by this statement from the New Jersey World Languages Curriculum Framework:

> The latest instructional technologies, particularly the most interactive technologies such as computer-assisted language learning and advanced telecommunications, enhance the possibilities of providing world languages for all students, while bringing languages and cultures into the classroom in an immediate and authentic way. Technology transforms the world languages classroom by recreating the multidimensional nature of language as it exists within the visual, social, and cultural world.
>
> (New Jersey Department of Education web site)

This multidimensional nature of language is nowhere better reflected than in the overarching goal areas and the individual Spanish Standards. Language is communication, but it is also culture; making connections and comparisons between other languages and one's own; and life-long language learning, which truly refers to language used in communities outside the academic environment.

NON-INTERNET TECHNOLOGY[3]

Following is a discussion of several technologies that do not require access to the Internet. These technologies can be used regularly to enhance Spanish instruction and address the Spanish Standards.

The technologies and products mentioned are meant to be a representation of those available to teachers, not necessarily an endorsement of the product or guarantee of the success of the technology.

Several commercially available programs for foreign languages (Atajo for Spanish, Système-D for French, and Quelle for German[4]) are designed to aid written production.[5] These programs assist language learners by providing a searchable grammar base (using grammatical topics such as future tense, adverbial clauses, conjunctions, etc.), verb conjugation assistance in all tenses, bilingual dictionaries (with two-way searches), and vocabulary support (words are clustered semantically; e.g., food, body parts, modes of transportation, hobbies, etc.). Students could be encouraged to use this software to write on a given theme or topic, thus addressing at least the three Communication standards. An assignment to write to partner classrooms in a target language country expands the activity to touch on Standards 5.1 and 5.2: using the language beyond the boundaries of the classroom and hopefully instilling a desire for life-long learning in the students.

As an ancillary to regular computer composition, without using one of the aforementioned writing assistants, foreign language spell checking software is available commercially. Alkai Proofing Tools for Office 97[6] provide spell checking functions in various languages. In addition, some word processing programs automatically provide some language support; this can be accomplished by changing the language designation in the configuration settings (e.g., Microsoft Word).

CD-ROMs as regular ancillaries accompany nearly every new textbook coming out these days. Teachers should investigate these materials carefully—in fact, approach them as a terrible language learner, make lots of typical mistakes, and see what sort of feedback and guidance the programs offer. Then take that information into consideration when deciding whether or not the CD really adds to the program in a meaningful way. Teachers and students can also make their own CDs with their own materials. A CD is merely a blank storage medium, just like a floppy disk or the hard drive of the computer. Any type of digital file desired can be put on a CD, including text files, audio files, video files, image files, PowerPoint Presentations, HTML files, etc. As long as the file format is digital, it can be burned on a blank CD.

Students using CDs that are ancillaries to a given textbook series are using technology to address several standards simultaneously, which is as it should be. Activities contained on such CDs frequently provide the opportunity for students to interpret target language input of both a written and an aural nature, and also offer a rich cultural context in which the students can study the language. Standards 1.2 (Interpretive Communication), 2.1 (Practices of Culture), and 2.2 (Products of Culture) clearly come into play by using these CDs.

For the more intrepid among us or for those who simply want to have a hand in designing the activities their students use, there are authoring programs. These programs typically are organized into templates that include a variety of answer/response formats such as multiple choice, true/false, matching, cloze, scrambled words or sentences. Many of the programs provide for inclusion of multimedia—digitized video and audio. Teacher authors can then tailor-make activities that coordinate with the text or topics they are covering in their classes. Examples of these authoring programs are Libra (on Macintosh videodisc at Southwest Texas University), WinCalis (Computer Assisted Language Instruction for Windows—at Duke University, on Windows platform—that supports all world language texts), Dasher (University of Iowa; both platforms), the xMediaEngine Template Series (Middlebury College, Macintosh), and there are several more.

Commercial presentational software is also available and includes such programs as Microsoft PowerPoint, Hyperstudio, KidPix, and Aldus Persuasion. These programs have the capability of combining text, graphics, and video and can be used to create rich cultural materials and presentations. While this software is not specifically designed for foreign language use, diacritics are available for Spanish.

When teachers use authoring tools or presentational software to create lessons or activities, or to communicate information to their students, they are directly tapping Standards 1.2 (Interpretive Communication) and 1.3 (Presentational Communication). Depending on the subject or goal of the lesson or activity, many additional Standards could be addressed. For example, a lesson on the differences between the use of *tú* and *usted* touches on Standards 2.1 (Practices of Culture), 4.1 (Language Comparisons), and 4.2 (Cultural Comparisons).

These are just some of the many non-Internet technologies available to us at this time. They offer exciting possibilities for using authentic materials, engaging our students in meaningful activities, designing customized lessons to meet our specific learning objectives, and providing foreign language course options that otherwise might not be available.

INTERNET TECHNOLOGY

Just as non-Internet technologies have opened up new options for language instruction and learning, so have Internet technologies. More than ever, the Internet has connected us to all parts of the earth, giving new meaning to the phrases "global community" and "shrinking world." Below are several of these Internet technologies and ways in which they might well be put to use in the Spanish classroom.

Electronic mail, or e-mail, is pervasive in our lives today. It is also perhaps the technology that most teachers have used first in their classrooms. *Virtual Connections*, a volume edited by Mark Warschauer in 1995, contains 125 examples of projects that foreign language teachers have carried out in their classrooms, using e-mail and other various electronic communications technologies. E-mail provides an easy way for language students to practice their target language skills, whether it be with other language learners through a discussion format; their teacher, through dialog journaling; or even native speakers, through a penpal or keypal arrangement or project (Knight; LeLoup, "But I Only Have E-mail"). Standards that are addressed by students using e-mail to connect with native speakers, establish partnerships between classrooms, interchange information and cultural knowledge, and make new friends around the world include the seven within the categories of Communication, Cultures, and Communities.

Electronic discussion lists and Usenet groups abound on the Internet. A list is a discussion group on a topic of common interest to the subscribers. Literally thousands of lists exist on the Internet and, in actuality, hundreds are dedicated, or related in some way, to foreign language learning and instruction (Bedell). E-mail lists can be valuable resources for teachers. Through participation in the discussions with others that subscribe to these lists, teachers can become involved in a professional dialogue about any aspect of teaching or language they wish. Exchanges are plentiful and range from theoretical discussions to practical suggestions for enhancing classroom activities, to comments on textbook series, to advice about travel companies for student trips. This collegial exchange is a way for Spanish teachers to participate in on-going professional development and networking (LeLoup & Ponterio).

In particular, the singleton teachers mentioned previously — those who live in small towns or areas where direct Spanish influence is relatively inaccessible — and those whose districts cannot, or do not, fund conference attendance, find participation in e-mail discussion groups to be a wonderful way of ameliorating their isolation and staying current with developments in the field. Many lists routinely post announcements of local, state, regional, and national conferences as well as other professional development opportunities. Some language-specific lists will help improve the language competence and cultural knowledge of its members through regular "conversations" with native speakers, through which linguistic and cultural comparisons are also noted and often discussed.

One discussion list formed particularly for teachers and speakers of Spanish is ESPAN-L. Discussion includes a wide range of topics from cultural notes to grammatical points. Native and non-native speakers ask and receive language-related information on this list. To subscribe, send a message to the list subscription address (listserv@uacsc2.albany.edu) saying SUBSCRIBE ESPAN-L, and add your first name and last name.

Another electronic discussion list that exists for anyone interested in issues related to language teaching and learning is FLTEACH. This list was formed in 1994 and has over 4000 subscribers from more than 50 countries, with primary subscriptions from the United States. More than twenty languages are represented on the list, and the discussions center on topics of interest to all foreign language educators. In addition, all list discussions are archived for easy reference, and FLTEACH also has a page of "FAQs" (frequently discussed topics) that categorizes many popular and recurring discussions on the list. To subscribe, send a message saying "SUBSCRIBE FLTEACH firstname last-name" to the list subscription address (listserv@listserv.acsu. buffalo.edu).[7] By taking advantage of the opportunities available through participation in electronic discussion lists, teachers increase their own target language and cultural knowledge and abilities. By extension, when they utilize the information they have gained through using this technology, they are addressing the standards in their daily teaching.

An alternative to joining e-mail lists is participation in USENET newsgroups, if your service provider offers that option. Postings are read via a news reader, which keeps track of what messages have or have not been read in a particular thread or discussion topic. You can log on, select a thread, find the new messages, and read them. You can also initiate threads and post responses, much as you would post something on a bulletin board (another name frequently used for these groups). Again, Spanish language and even country-specific newsgroups would be of particular interest to Spanish teachers. Such newsgroup headers as *soc.culture.latin-america, soc.culture.mexican,* and *soc.culture.spain* can easily be found using a newsgroup reader. Efforts to meet the standards goal area of Culture are clearly enhanced by the use of this technology.

Conferencing systems are also available through the Internet via commercial packaging. Such systems as Daedalus or the FirstClass Conferencing8 system allow teachers to set up private discussion groups limited to a particular class. These systems are relatively easy to administer and tend to be of the client-server variety. These systems also typically support the extended character sets so necessary for foreign language exchange, whereas this support is rare in newsgroups. Another advantage of these conferencing systems is their moderation by a teacher, who can regulate and direct the discussion according to the class needs and curricular demands. While these systems are typically meant to be for asynchronous discussion (participants are not all present concurrently but can respond to messages posted at a later time), they may have provision for synchronous dialog exchange (participants communicate in a real-time setting). The Interchange portion of Daedalus is an example of this capability.

Video conferencing systems are also available, such as Microsoft NetMeeting and CUSeeMe. The latter software was developed by Cornell University in conjunction with White Pine Software as an endeavor to create affordable and workable desktop videoconferencing. MS NetMeeting software is available on the Internet as freeware but CUSeeMe software must now be purchased.[9] With these programs and some sort of digital camera, you can see and talk to someone at the same time. Obviously, this is optimal communication—with body language, facial expressions, intonations—everything one can get live except being there. (One probably should not use this on a bad hair day!)

Opportunities for synchronous target language conversations are also numerous. Internet Relay Chat, or IRC, is one such application. IRC is a very popular program that presents a series of "channels," rather like a CB. By entering a channel, users can "talk" to all of the other people on the channel, no matter where they are in the world. Everything typed by any participant will be seen instantly by all of the other people there. Channel names usually reflect the topics discussed, so entering a channel called "español" might be interesting for a Spanish class, especially if an appointment has been made to meet some other *hispanohablantes* there at a specific time. A quick look at the list of topics available as channels in IRC might convince teachers that it is not a good place to leave students unsupervised, but IRC does have a great potential for worldwide, interactive communication. It also holds promise for small-scale Spanish conversation practice. Teachers can create private channels for individual classes with the software available. Students participating in target language interchanges via conferencing software are addressing the Communication standards throughout the activity. Depending on the interlocutor and the task assigned, several other standards could be implemented in a synchronous or asynchronous conference exchange in the target language.

MUDs (Multi-User Dimensions), MOOs (MUD Object-Oriented), and MUSHes (Multi-User Shared Hallucinations) are primarily used for role playing games. A player who enters one of these "places" takes a nickname and then proceeds to interact with the other people there according to rules that can be quite different at each site. Several language MOOs have been established where students can interact in the target language. The students themselves create a virtual environment incorporating aspects of the target culture. Of note are the MOO Francais and Mundohispano, two well-run and highly regulated MOOs for language learners.[10] Many native speakers frequent these MOOs, and language learners can get much good and authentic target language conversation practice by participating.

Finally we get to the World Wide Web. One might ask why teachers would want to use the WWW for language instruction and how it can help to address the Spanish Standards. Among the most compelling reasons for Spanish teachers to use the Web in teaching toward the implementation of the five goal areas are the following:

- **Access to authentic and timely materials in the target language.** Teachers and language learners can keep up daily with happenings around the globe and interact with native speakers in just about any language desired. (Communication, Culture, Connections, Comparisons, Communities)

- **Access to a wealth of cultural information.** Given the large number of Spanish-speaking countries, most teachers are hard-pressed to be cultural experts on more than a few at most. The Web is an immense resource for teachers and students to research nearly any topic. (Culture, Connections, Comparisons, Communities)

- **Maintenance/improvement of language skills.** Teachers and students can rely on target language input from Internet sources in the form of streaming audio and video broadcasts. (Communication, Culture, Communities)

- **Languages across the curriculum (LAC).** T
  a real boon to these programs. Now it is eas
  materials on all kinds of subjects on the Inter
  one needs to employ foreign language skills
  information. What better reinforcement for t
  their students how their Spanish skills will se
  future? (Connections, Comparisons, Commur

- **Motivation/Appeal to MTV learners.** Whether we like it or
  not, our student population is more and more visually oriented.
  Students who have been weaned on MTV, Nintendo, Sega, and
  myriad video and electronic games are simply not very excited
  by mere textbooks, no matter how colorful they have become.
  Many students also are quite computer-literate, and they enjoy
  and prefer the challenge of finding Spanish language
  information on the web to filling out worksheets, writing in
  workbooks, and reading from textbooks. Still others might not
  feel at ease using the technology but recognize it as an
  important component of their education, perhaps even more so
  than their foreign language experience. Motivation for
  language study can benefit from the association with new
  technological tools, showing the students that language is also a
  tool for the future. (Communication, Connections,
  Communities)

- **Interactivity.** While MTV fan status may seem to belie this, our
  students are truly interested in activities that are interactive, in
  which they can participate themselves instead of just being
  passive learners. Technology researchers have also begun
  noticing that children who surf the web are reading. This alone
  can be a benefit in our less literate society. The basic
  information might be the same and the knowledge gained in the
  end identical, but students will arguably opt for gleaning the
  facts from an interactive session on the web over simply reading
  them on the printed page. Carefully designed lessons using
  materials from the Internet can reinforce this interactivity, and
  thus active participation on the part of students, hopefully
  leading to enhanced language learning. (Communication,
  Communities)

The key concept underlying the use of materials from the
Internet is that the lessons and activities must be standards-based
and curriculum-driven. Spanish teachers need to examine the
curricula particular to their own language courses, select certain
primary concepts and foci; design the curriculum using the Spanish

...ards as a guide; and then select the materials, tools, and ...ethodologies to deliver it. We need to know how to incorporate technology resources into our lessons so that they complement our objectives and goals and facilitate their achievement. In sum, the resources obtained through communications technologies should be selected only with the express purpose of improving teaching and learning.

EXAMPLES OF THE IMPLEMENTATION OF THE STANDARDS THROUGH TECHNOLOGY

The following section will suggest some technologies that could be used in addressing the objectives of each of the standards. In addition, some technologies will be suggested as examples for accomplishing activities given in the Progress Indicators for each age grouping. It is important to note that addressing one Standard frequently entails addressing several others simultaneously. For example, an activity or lesson whose primary aim is the communication of an aspect of the target language culture will most likely also address standards in the goal areas of Communication, Comparisons, and perhaps Connections and Communities as well. The standards do not exist separately in isolation but rather are interrelated; teaching to the standards in an integrated fashion is the optimal approach.

Goal 1   Communication
Communicate in Spanish

Standard 1.1 Students engage in conversation, provide and obtain information, express feelings and emotions, and exchange opinions. (Interpersonal mode)

A veritable plethora of technologies exists to facilitate this Standard. Spanish teachers want their students conversing in Spanish, expressing their opinions, thoughts, and feelings; in other words, the goal is to have them engaging in real-life conversations in Spanish. What better way than to put them in contact with native speakers or other second-language learners of Spanish all over the world? By using such communications technologies as e-mail, IRC, Usenet groups, and MOOs, Spanish learners can regularly communicate with a variety of interlocutors. This use of technology literally brings the world to our classroom. Students could be asked to conduct a survey of native speakers about a cultural point discussed in class. Students would use the technologies to contact people from different Hispanic origins, survey them on the topic, summarize, and report back to the class.

Teachers could arrange keypal exchanges with classrooms in a Spanish-speaking country or even with classroom learners of Spanish in another part of the United States.

Sample Progress Indicator - Grade 4

- Students ask and answer questions about very familiar topics, such as family, school events, and celebrations, in person or via short letters, e-mail, audio, or video tapes.[11]

Sample Progress Indicator - Grade 8

- Students use Spanish in group activities such as "town meetings" and advice columns in which they develop and propose solutions to issues and problems related to the school or community. They write their columns using writing assistance software such as Atajo.

Sample Progress Indicator - Grade 12

- Through Spanish-language chat rooms or news groups, students use Spanish to exchange and support their opinions and individual perspectives with peers and/or other Spanish-speakers on a variety of topics dealing with contemporary and historical issues, perhaps representing opposing views of a political or historical issue such as an indigenous perspective on the European "discovery" of the "New World." Information is gleaned from target-language newspapers via the WWW and from native speakers.

Sample Progress Indicators - Grade 16

- Using the WWW to access Spanish-language newspapers and authentic advertisements for employment and other opportunities, students search for jobs in their fields of study, responding to classified ads
- Using the WWW to access professionals in Spanish speaking countries; e-mail for contact with native speakers; and writing assistant software, students use Spanish orally and in writing to communicate with people already employed in their field of study by writing letters of inquiry for positions and/or participating in simulated job interviews.

Standard 1.2   Students understand and interpret written and spoken Spanish on a variety of topics. (Interpretive mode)

- Second language learners need access to authentic materials covering a broad range of topics in order to experience learning in context. Fortunately, access to this sort of information is readily available from a variety of sources. Many language learning and textbook-specific CD-ROMs contain digitized multimedia input that is both written and spoken. The Internet can readily provide a wealth of information in the written form of on-line daily or weekly newspapers, journals, and magazines from the Hispanic world. Aural input can come from synchronous and asynchronous broadcasts from radio and television stations throughout the global Latin community. Students can listen to native speakers from many different Spanish-speaking countries and learn to interpret input containing different accents, vocabulary, and even registers. A very sophisticated project could include differentiating among native speaker accents, depending on the country of origin. Students could be asked to research varying viewpoints among native speakers of different countries on a world event.

Sample Progress Indicator - Grade 4

- Students interpret gestures, intonation, and other visual or auditory clues in Spanish-language visual media such as videos, films, and television programs.

Sample Progress Indicator - Grade 8

- Students understand the main themes and significant details of writings on topics from other subjects and products of the cultures as found in newspapers, magazines, e-mail, the Internet, the World Wide Web, or other sources in Spanish.

Sample Progress Indicator - Grade 12

- Students demonstrate an understanding of the principal elements of non-fiction articles such as those found in newspapers, magazines, and e-mail, on topics of current and historical importance to Spanish speakers.

Sample Progress Indicator - Grade 16

- Students investigate the cultural basis of humor, using cartoons and comics found on the WWW in TL newspapers and magazines.

Standard 1.3 Students present information, concepts, and ideas in Spanish to an audience of listeners or readers on a variety of topics. (Presentational mode)

Students generally enjoy doing well-defined projects and frequently amaze their teachers with spurts of creativity and originality. Desktop publishing programs and presentational software can assist students in creating projects that communicate information in Spanish and allow them to demonstrate an understanding of the concepts that they have researched. Such programs include, but are not limited to, written expression in the language; indeed, they can include Spanish audio files recorded by the student or an outside source as well. Students could be asked to choose a Spanish-speaking country, research several common topics about that country (e.g., history, geography, politics, a cultural topic), and create a Hyperstudio project that communicates the highlights of the information found. The project could include graphics depicting the various topics covered and audio files with music and target language input describing the representations in the project. Students might also design and create a brochure advertising their particular country and present it as if they were travel agents.

Sample Progress Indicator - Grade 4

- Using software such as Hyperstudio and KidPix, students prepare illustrated stories about activities or events in their environment and share them with an audience such as the class.

Sample Progress Indicator - Grade 8

- Students prepare tape or video recorded messages on topics of personal interest to share locally or with school peers and/or members of the Spanish-speaking community, using culturally appropriate behavior or typical gestures.

Sample Progress Indicators - Grade 12

- Students summarize the content of an excerpt from cable television in Spanish in order to discuss the topics via e-mail with other speakers of the language.
- Students write a letter or an article describing and analyzing an issue for a Spanish-language student publication, using writing assistant software such as Atajo.

- Using the WWW to gain access to target cultural perspectives through newspaper reports or direct contact with native speakers, students prepare a research-based analysis of a current event or issue such as the World Cup finals or immigration, from the perspective of both U.S. and Hispanic cultures.

Sample Progress Indicator - Grade 16

- Students use desktop publishing software to develop brochures, prospectuses, or scientific reports for use in their fields of study.

Goal 2   Culture
Gain Knowledge and Understanding of Spanish-Speaking Cultures

Standard 2.1   Students demonstrate an understanding of the relationship between the practices and perspectives of Hispanic cultures.

How might students come in contact or become familiar with practices and perspectives of a culture, particularly if no native speakers are to be found in their vicinity? The WWW might be particularly useful here, or an electronic discussion group or even Usenet. The idea is to find a way to obtain cultural information that is not readily available. For example, a local newspaper briefly covers a fiesta in Spain called the Tomatina, with a photo and a two-line explanation of people throwing tomatoes at each other. Why do they do that? Is this an ancient ritual? A recently instituted practice? A long-standing tradition?

Students can use technology to survey native speakers on their attitudes toward a variety of practices, determining just how important these practices are in reality. By querying native speakers across generational lines, students may find differing and even changing perspectives. Just how important is it to kiss on both cheeks as a salutation, to greet everyone in the room individually, to use titles of address instead of personal names, etc.? Which Spanish-speaking countries use *tú* more than *usted*, and when precisely should that shift occur in personal relationships? Investigation of these cultural practices and perspectives can help to dispel or confirm stereotypes and/or cultural generalizations. Language learners can use the WWW to look up information on these happenings that most likely will not be in the encyclopedia. These activities also address Standard 3.2 by gathering information available only through the language being studied.   Again, technology can bring the world to our classroom, and difficulties caused by distance melt away.

Sample Progress Indicator - Grade 4

- Students observe, identify, and/or demonstrate simple patterns of behavior or interaction in various settings such as school, family, and the community within the context of Spanish-speakers, recognizing such things as who speaks first, who addresses whom first, and forms of address that demonstrate politeness, respect, and consideration for others. Sources of information may be CD-ROMS and videos, perhaps ancillary materials for textbooks series; and Spanish-language television programs and *telenovelas*.

Sample Progress Indicator - Grade 8

- Students vicariously participate in real or simulated age-appropriate cultural occurrences related to special events or personal occasions, such as saint's days and birthday celebrations, and graduation exercises, through discussions of these topics via e-mail contact with keypals.

Sample Progress Indicator - Grade 12

- Using information gained via WWW and contact with native speakers, students identify, analyze, and discuss various Hispanic patterns of behavior or interaction related to cultural perspectives that are typical of the diversity in Hispanic cultures, such as weddings, funerals, personal events, independence day observances, and national ceremonial events. Students then create PowerPoint presentations of comparisons of these cultural topics.

Sample Progress Indicator - Grade 16

- Students Gather information via the WWW to identify, analyze, and support or challenge positions that reflect current issues and events that affect the Hispanic community, such as the English Only movement, or the changes in economic patterns that threaten traditional ways of life. They organize a debate on the controversial topic.

Standard 2.2   Students demonstrate an understanding of the relationship between the products and perspectives of the different Hispanic cultures.

Culturally motivated videos and films are of significant help in addressing this Standard, primarily for their informational content, including visual representations of artifacts and products from Hispanic societies. The presence of a *molinillo* in a Mexican film could spark a discussion of the importance of this product that is representative of a rich cultural tradition. Describing it and how it works would be one thing, and quite another would be to see a *molinillo* being used to make *chocolate*. Likewise, a film snippet showing Argentines drinking *mate* from the traditional silver-encrusted gourds could be the basis for a discussion of differences between populations in South American countries, their heritage, and their customs. Often, we need only show very short segments of films to reap great cultural rewards from their content.

Sample Progress Indicator - Grade 4

- Students observe, identify and/or describe tangible products from Spanish-speaking cultures such as toys (*papeletas, títeres*), traditional and contemporary dress (*las molas de San Blas, los huipiles de Guatemala*), types of dwellings (*palacios, casas, chosas*), and staple foods (*arroz, frijoles* in Central America). They obtain information via videos illustrating these various aspects of the culture.

Sample Progress Indicator - Grade 8

- Using the WWW and videos, students search for, investigate, and identify the function of *artesanías*, which might include hand painted ceramics, serapes, baskets, jewelry, *molinillos* for making hot chocolate, and wooden and stone carvings as found within their homes and local communities. They may also contact native speakers for their particular perspectives on the meanings of these products.

Sample Progress Indicator - Grade 12

- Students explore the relationships among the products, practices, and perspectives of Spanish speakers as indicated in formal documents such as the Spanish Constitution of 1978; in political cartoons; and in product advertising unique to the region being studied, such as the Maja health and beauty care products of Spain. Students investigate these relationships by participation through postings to cultural newsgroups and via discussions in MOOs.

Sample Progress Indicator - Grade 16

- Students contact native speakers via chat rooms to get differing perspectives and participate appropriately in discussions with Spanish speakers about literary, social, economic, political, and other topics that might be controversial, such as social classes and the extent to which they are depicted realistically in film, literature, and the news media.

Goal 3   Connections
Connect with Other Disciplines and Acquire Information

Standard 3.1 Students reinforce and further their knowledge of other disciplines through Spanish.

This standard affords an excellent opportunity for collaboration among teachers of different disciplines. One obvious meeting point would be between the metric system and the measurement system used in the United States. Most students in the United States are not at all familiar or comfortable with the metric system and find it difficult to relate even to temperatures given in Celsius. A collaborative project between the Math teacher, the Geography or Science teacher, and the Spanish teacher could involve learning the metric system and doing daily weather checks in different Spanish-speaking countries. This information is readily found on the WWW and in Spanish-language newspapers published on-line. Students could be asked to do mini-weather reports on a given city or region, complete with temperatures in Celsius and tourism implications. The Art and Spanish teachers might choose to combine forces in a unit on Spanish artists, complete with a virtual tour of the Prado. Each student could be asked to concentrate on a single artist, investigating the life, background, style, and works of the individual. The student could then write a report using Atajo and, as the culmination of the project, create and present to the class the salient points of the report using PowerPoint.

Sample Progress Indicator - Grade 4

- Students create simple Hyperstudio presentations with text and drawings to demonstrate in Spanish an understanding about concepts learned in other subject areas, such as the categorization of animals by their habitats; this may include concepts such as weather, mathematics, measurements, and geography.[12]

Sample Progress Indicator - Grade 8

- Students comprehend articles accessed on the WWW or short culturally-based videos in Spanish on topics being studied in other classes, such as current sports events, volcanic eruptions and other natural disasters, and national patriotic celebrations (e.g., independence day in various countries).

Sample Progress Indicator - Grade 12

- Students acquire information from a variety of sources written in Spanish about a topic being studied in a range of school subjects; for example, they use an essay on European architecture of the 16th century and an Internet tour of the Prado Museum as they study the Renaissance in an interdisciplinary unit.

Sample Progress Indicator - Grade 16

- Students use Spanish language resources available through electronic means, such as chat rooms, e-mail, and Internet, to gather information in Spanish on the work and knowledge base of professionals in their own fields of study.

Standard 3.2   Students acquire information and recognize the distinctive viewpoints that are available only through the Spanish language and its many cultures.

Frequently, our students are amazed to find that everyone in the world does not think precisely as they do here in the United States. In order to reinforce this more global way of thinking about different topics, students could be asked to do an Internet search for organizations that have branches in different countries and to investigate the stance a particular country or organization might take on a global topic. One such topic that would be germane to the Spanish curriculum and culture is animal rights, bullfighting, and the Society for the Protection and Care of Animals. Students could be asked to find examples of differing perspectives on Bullfighting as a sport, as an art, and as cruelty to animals and try to understand the viewpoints of Spanish-speaking people toward this controversial topic. Another subject that is frequently surrounded by controversy is the "celebration" or recognition of Columbus Day or *El día de la raza*. Students could investigate differing viewpoints on this day by accessing the WWW and seeking articles written about it in Spanish-speaking newspapers and magazines. They could also query native speakers in chat rooms and on newsgroups for their personal opinions regarding this date in history and subsequent events.

Sample Progress Indicator - Grade 4

- Students read, listen to, and talk about the cultural bases of age-appropriate school content, folk tales, short stories, poems, and songs written for native speakers of Spanish. This material can be found on CDs and perhaps in digitized video recordings on the WWW.

Sample Progress Indicator - Grade 8

- Students use the WWW to search for sources about the United States intended for same-age speakers of Spanish and analyze different perspectives on contemporary issues of concern and/or interest (e.g., articles on U.S. celebrities and famous persons from Hispanic countries in the United States; news reports on current events in the United States; television commercials that advertise U.S.-made products for local consumption in other countries).

Sample Progress Indicator - Grade 12

- Students use a variety of sources intended for same-age speakers of Spanish to prepare reports on topics of personal interest, or those with which they have limited previous experience, and compare these to information obtained on the same topics written in English (e.g., obituary announcements from several different countries' newspapers — easily obtained through the Internet).

Sample Progress Indicator - Grade 16

- Students use information available only in Spanish, acquired through the WWW by using Spanish search engines, in comparisons with information on the same topics available in English, and analyze the different perspectives and/or biases shown in the sources. Examples might be the English Only movement, conditions of migrant workers, indigenous movements and human rights, or bilingual education.

Goal 4   Comparisons
Develop Insights into the Nature of Language and Culture

Standard 4.1 Students demonstrate understanding of the nature of language through comparisons between Spanish and English.

Often students ask questions about vocabulary that is simply not within the lexicon of the teacher. No translation might be available for a given phrase or idea, or a radically different way to say what the student wants to express might be most acceptable. One example that frequently arises in Spanish class is a request for the translation of "cheerleader." As this concept does not even exist in many Hispanic countries, the teacher must explain such things as cultural differences in school systems and the irrelevance of one-to-one word equivalents in this circumstance. Some Hispanic countries do have cheerleaders but they use different vocabulary words to express this idea. This gets even further into cultural differences and can be quite surprising for many students. This sort of lexical information can be discovered via electronic discussion lists or newsgroups by sending or posting a query to other participants, and on-line dictionaries on the WWW—all of which can be very helpful for the Spanish teacher.

Sample Progress Indicator - Grade 4

- Students study idiomatic expressions in English and in Spanish, and explain how idiomatic expressions work in general (e.g., *tomar el pelo* - to pull one's leg; *llover a cántaros* - to rain buckets). They use presentational software to illustrate these idioms and then communicate their ideas to the class.

Sample Progress Indicator - Grade 8

- Students use writing programs and proofing tools to demonstrate an awareness of grammatical gender in Spanish.

Sample Progress Indicator - Grade 12

- To demonstrate an awareness that there are phrases and idioms that do not translate directly from Spanish to English or vice-versa, such as *tomar una decisión* or *hacer pedazos* in Spanish; and to rain cats and dogs or to eat like a horse in English, students use writing software to create skits illustrating problems of direct translation; then videotape the skits for parents' night or a PTO presentation.

Sample Progress Indicator - Grade 16

- Students create a PowerPoint presentation to illustrate what they have learned about register differences; for example, the importance of tailoring their language to professional vs. social contexts and purposes.

Standard 4.2 Students demonstrate understanding of the concept of culture through comparisons between Hispanic cultures and their own.

Students can become aware of many cultural differences by viewing films and videos, listening to music, and reading authentic texts, among many other activities. One use of technology to expand cultural understanding revolves around the celebration of the *quinceañera*. After reading a brief paragraph in Spanish on this topic in the textbook, students can go to the web and search for more information about this celebration. They might find differences among Hispanic countries, and they will most certainly find both differences and similarities between the *quinceañera* and the *sweet sixteen* party from the United States. Students could also be encouraged to discuss this topic with their e-mail partners in another country or a friend they have met in a language MOO or IRC chat room.

Sample Progress Indicator - Grade 4

- Using information derived from CDs, students compare and contrast intangible products of Hispanic cultures and their own, such as *leyendas*; team cheers (*A la bi, a la ba, a la sim, bum, ba*); children's rhymes (*Tortillas, tortillas, para mamá…*); and songs (*Arroz con leche; Naranja dulce*).

Sample Progress Indicator - Grade 8

- Students demonstrate an awareness that they, too, have a culture, by comparing sample daily activities in Hispanic cultures and their own (e.g., mealtimes as family events including *sobremesa*; dating customs in both cultures; the influence of sports heroes and other cultural icons on aspects of daily life in the United States). Students contact native speakers via e-mail or newsgroups or query native speakers in MOOs regarding these similarities and differences and then write in Spanish about cultural differences using writing assistant software.

Sample Progress Indicator - Grade 12

- Students access the WWW and CDs to hear regional music and learn about its origin and to identify variations in rhythms instrumentation as reflections of local resources and history (*el güiro* in Puerto Rico, *el cuatro* in Venezuela, *el charango* and *la flauta* in the Andean region, *la marimba* in Central America).

Sample Progress Indicator - Grade 16

- Students search for official Spanish-language sites via the Internet to obtain information about cultural institutions, such as government, schools, and religion, and identify similarities and differences between Hispanic institutions and those of the United States.

Goal 5   Communities
Participate in Multilingual Communities
at Home and Around the World

Standard 5.1 Students use Spanish both within and beyond the school setting.

Many students in the United States have fairly easy access to Spanish input outside the classroom. The growing numbers of Spanish-speaking people in this country are accompanied by the widespread availability of authentic materials and input that students encounter in most large metropolitan areas and, indeed, in nearly every state in some form. Students can readily find Spanish-language CDs by current hit singers and groups (Selena, Gloria Estefan and the Miami Sound Machine, Ricky Martin, Luis Miguel). Many of these are quite popular among English-speaking students, thus providing expanded use of Spanish outside the school setting. In addition, movies produced in Spanish-speaking countries are frequently available for rental at local stores. Students may also easily find and participate in Spanish-speaking communities on-line.

Sample Progress Indicator – Grade 4

- Students convey messages to Spanish speakers in person and by telephone, letters, e-mail, audio cassettes, and video tapes.

Sample Progress Indicator – Grade 8

- Students interview Spanish-speaking members of their local community to learn how they use Spanish in their various fields of work. Students use tape recorders to capture rich Spanish-language input from the interviews.

Sample Progress Indicator - Grade 12

- Using writing assistants and proofing tools, students create an interesting newsletter for a partner classroom in a Spanish-speaking country.

Sample Progress Indicator – Grade 16

- Students participate in public access television programs, local radio broadcasts, and other public speaking opportunities in Spanish.

Standard 5.2   Students show evidence of becoming life-long learners by using Spanish for personal enjoyment and enrichment.

Students who enjoy studying the language and are motivated to do so will most likely benefit from increased language use within the classroom as well as outside the school setting. Students may opt to see a Spanish film or attend a rock concert by a popular Spanish-speaking musician. Hopefully, students will also realize that they can continue to maintain their language skills by accessing daily target language input from the web, CDs, videos, films, cable TV, and the like.

Sample Progress Indicator - Grade 4

- Students read materials in Spanish (*cuentos infantiles*, children's web pages, *leyendas*), view children's programs in Spanish on cable television, and listen to music CDs from Spanish-speaking countries for personal enjoyment.

Sample Progress Indicator - Grade 8

- For personal entertainment, students listen to CDs with Hispanic music; sing; and play music from Spanish-speaking countries.

Sample Progress Indicator – Grade 12

- Students continue to learn more about personal interests by consulting various Spanish references, such as Spanish websites on the Internet, *periódicos y revistas*, and Spanish-Spanish dictionaries.

Sample Progress Indicator - Grade 16

- Students use electronic correspondence, such as e-mail and chat rooms, to make and maintain relationships with Spanish speakers.

In the Spanish standards document, many learning scenarios are given to assist teachers in addressing the standards. Nearly every scenario employs one or more technologies to effect the objectives and outcomes of the lesson. In addition, teachers who are savvy in the ways of web design are beginning to make Standards-based lessons available on the WWW for their colleagues to use.[13]

CONCLUSION

As we have seen, foreign language teachers have been using many different kinds of "older" technology for years. Many of us are beginning to use newer technologies that are presently available, and our future will most likely include currently emerging technologies (such as more sophisticated video conferencing programs or voice recognition software) and even those not yet developed. Technology is a phenomenon that is not going away. It is present in nearly all aspects of our lives, and very importantly and usefully, in our work. The technologies that we now take for granted were hailed as great discoveries at their beginning. The advent of newer and more sophisticated communications technologies must be considered in the same light. They bring the world to our classroom and make language learning real for our students. Technology can assist teachers in providing target language input, interaction, and cultural context, all of which are key elements in successful language instruction and learning. Language experiences that reach around the world, made possible by myriad technologies at our disposal, are exemplars of language in context that promotes second language acquisition. These technologies can refresh and energize us and motivate and excite our learners. Most of all, these technologies enable us to address the Spanish standards in an efficient, effective, interesting, and complete manner. Spanish teachers must first make pedagogically sound decisions about the implementation of these technologies in their curriculum and then use them to maximize Spanish-language input and output. Clearly, the role of technology is increasingly key in meeting the goals of Communication, Culture, Connections, Comparisons, and Communities.

NOTES

1. For more information on the New Jersey World Languages Curriculum Framework, see the following site:
http://www.state.nj.us/njded/frameworks/worldlanguages/

2. For more information on the NETS project, see http://cnets.iste.org/.

3. For more on non-internet technologies, see Earp; Martinez-Lage and Herren.

4. These writing assistants are available from Heinle and Heinle Publishers.

5. Some preliminary research studies have shown some positive results such as students producing more text and students generating more and better ideas when using the writing assistant than when writing with the more traditional means of paper and pencil (Scott).

6. These proofing tools are available from Microsoft.

7. For more information on FLTEACH, its archives and ancillaries, please see the FLTEACH home page: http://www.cortland.edu/flteach/

8. Daedalus software is available from The Daedalus Group, Inc. (http://www.daedalus.com/), and FirstClass can be obtained by contacting Centrinity (formerly SoftArc), Inc. (http://www.centrinity.com)

9. Microsoft NetMeeting can be downloaded free from the Microsoft homepage (http://www.microsoft.com). To obtain CUSeeMe software, contact CUseeMe Networks (formerly White Pine Software) (http://www.cuseeme.com).

10. Information for accessing Mundohispano, plus links to explanations of MOOs, can be found at the Mundohispano homepage (http://www.umsl.edu/~moosproj/mundo.html).

11. For examples of comprehensive projects employing technology that simultaneously address several goal areas (Communication, Cultures, Connections, Communities), please see Doloff; Shelley.

12. For an excellent example of a project that illustrates several Standards, including Connections, please see Pastorek.

13. For examples of Standards-based lessons using several different communications technologies, please see: http://www.cortland.edu/flteach/methods/obj4/intro4.html (LeLoup, "Communications Technology Module").

WORKS CITED

Bedell, David. Review of electronic lists for language learning. *Athelstan* 5 (1993):13-15.

Brzezowski, Edward H. "New Jersey Core Curriculum Content Standards: Integration of Technology in the Classroom." Last revised 4/23/98. http://www.gti.net/ebrzez/Technology/Core-Tech/core_tech.html (10 July, 1999)

Corder, S. Pitt. "The Significance of Learners' Errors." *International Review of Applied Linguistics* 5 (1967):161-69.

Doloff, Deby. "Te quiero, Tito." *Learning Languages* 4.3 (1999), 21-23.

Doughty, Catherine, and Teresa Pica. "'Information Gap' Tasks: Do They Facilitate Second Language Acquisition?" *TESOL Quarterly* 20 (1986):305-25.

Earp, Samantha. "More Than Just the Internet: Technology for Language Teaching." ERIC Digest, December 1997.

Ellis, Rod. *Understanding Second Language Acquisition.* Oxford, UK: Oxford University Press, 1985.

_____. *The Study of Second Language Acquisition.* Oxford: Oxford University Press, 1994.

Ervin, Gerard L. "Can Technology Fulfill its Promise?" *IALL Journal* 26.2 (1993):7-16.

Gardner, Robert. Social Psychology and Second Language Learning: The Role of Attitude and Motivation. London: Edward Arnold, 1985.

Gardner, Robert, and Wallace E. Lambert. *Attitudes and Motivation in Second Language Learning.* Rowley, MA: Newbury House, 1972.

Garrett, Nina. "Language Pedagogy and Effective Technology Use." *Applied Language Learning* 2.2 (1991):1-14.

_____. "Technology in the Service of Language Learning: Trends and Issues." *Modern Language Journal* 75 (1991):74-101.

International Society for Technology in Education (ISTE). *National Educational Technology Standards for Students.* National Educational Technology Standards (NETS) Project. http://cnets.iste.org/ (10 July, 1999).

_____. "Standards Projects." http://www.iste.org/Standards/ (10 July, 1999).

_____. *Connecting Curriculum and Technology.* Eugene, OR: ISTE, 2000.

Knight, Susan. "Making Authentic Cultural and Linguistic Connections." *Hispania* 77 (1994):288-94.

Lambert, Wallace E., Robert Gardner, et al. "A Study of the Roles of Attitudes and Motivation in Second-language Learning." *Readings in the Sociology of Language.* Ed. Joshua Fishman. The Hague: Mouton, 1968. 473-491.

LeLoup, Jean W. "But I Only Have E-mail — What Can I do?" *Learning Languages* 2.2 (1996):10-15

_____. "Communications Technology Module for the Foreign Language Methods Course." http://www.cortland.edu/flteach/methods/main.html (1997)

LeLoup, Jean W. and Robert Ponterio. "Networking with Foreign Language Colleagues: Professional Development on the Internet." *Northeast Conference Newsletter* 37 (Winter 1995):6-10.

Long, Michael. "Input and Second Language Acquisition Theory." *Input in Second Language Acquisition.* Eds. Susan Gass and Carolyn Madden. Rowley, MA: Newbury House, 1985.

Martínez-Lage, Ana, and David Herren. "Challenges and Opportunities: Curriculum Pressures in the Technological Present." *The Coming of Age of the Profession: Issues and Emerging Ideas for the Teaching of Foreign Languages.* Eds. Jane Harper, Madeleine Lively, and Mary Williams. Boston, MA: Heinle & Heinle Publishers, 1998. 141-167.

McLaughlin, Barry. *Theories of Second Language Learning.* London: Edward Arnold, 1987.

National Standards in Foreign Language Education Project. *Standards for Foreign Language Learning in the 21st Century.* Lawrence, KS: Allen, 1999.

New Jersey Department of Education. "World Languages Curriculum Framework." http://www.state.nj.us/njded/frameworks/worldlanguages/ (10 July, 1999)

Pastorek, Marcia. "Tech Frience: Integrating Foreign Language and Science through Technology." *Learning Languages* 5.1 (Fall 1999): 23-26.

Pitkoff, Evan, and Elizabeth Roosen. "New Technology, New Attitudes Provide Language Instruction." *NASSP Bulletin* (September 1994):36-43.

Salaberry, M. Rafael. "A theoretical foundation for the development of pedagogical tasks in computer mediated communication." *CALICO Journal* 14.1 (1996):5-34.

Scott, M. Virginia. *Rethinking Foreign Language Writing.* Boston: Heinle & Heinle Publishers, 1996.

Seelye, H. Ned. *Teaching Culture: Strategies for Intercultural Communication.* 3rd edition. Lincolnwood, IL: National Textbook Company, 1993.

Seliger, Herbert. "Psycholinguistic Issues in Second Language Acquisition." *Issues in Second Language Acquisition: Multiple perspectives.* Ed. Leslie Beebe. New York: Newbury House, 1988.

Selinker, Larry. "Interlanguage." *International Review of Applied Linguistics* 10 (1972): 209-31.

Shelley, Janine O. "Minneapolis and Brittany: Children Bridge Geographical and Social Differences through Technology." *Learning Languages* 2.1 (1996):3-11.

Warschauer, Mark. *Virtual Connections.* University of Hawaii Press, 1996.

Zhao, Yong. "Language Learning on the World Wide Web: Toward a Framework of Network Based CALL." *CALICO Journal* 14.1 (1996):37-51.

The Standards And The University Spanish/Portuguese Curriculum

Frank W. Medley, Jr.
West Virginia University

Carmen C. Tesser
University of Georgia

*Current language acquisition theory claims
that we acquire language...when we understand
what people tell us or what we read,
when we are absorbed in the message.*
(Stephen D. Krashen 1997)

*The phrase "Loving words" may be read as
"words of love" or as an activity in which we, students and
teachers, become aware of the extraordinary adventure
we are living in and through languages.*
(Elaine Marks 1997)

*Instead of despair, we need to face the fact that books
and rhetoric no longer represent the sole indexes of
literacy as they did in the last two centuries. We need
to remember that language use still does.*
(Janet Swaffar 1998)

*Besides, teaching isn't the inculcation of authoritative,
received opinion but the opposite: helping students to
read carefully yet raise questions, to develop
a conscious skepticism even toward what the
teacher and great works seem to assert.*
(Edward W. Said 1999)

> *The question underlying this discussion may actually be,*
> *what should the nature and structure of current*
> *language departments be?*
> (Bill VanPatten 1999)

> *Standards have defined the agenda for the next decade – and beyond.*
> (June Phillips 1999)

We open this discussion by presenting six points of view from the field. Our purpose in posing these issues is twofold. First, these comments and other recent developments point to a time of critical reflection from all of us involved in the education enterprise. Second, the six colleagues quoted above represent many perspectives about where we are and where we should be in the post-secondary context with respect to language, literature, and culture. We want to emphasize here the multiplicity of views about the future of our profession. Depending on the reader's background and context (e.g., second language acquisition, literary studies, cultural studies, linguistics, or foreign language education), these words bring to mind different images, indeed, different "meanings." One of our goals is to promote dialogue among our readers in an effort to identify our commonalties as well as begin to understand our differences. In other words, our ultimate goal is to open communication among our many cultures to foster connections and comparisons within our communities.

We can no longer look at these issues as a "we-they" proposition: the Standards give us a framework with which to engage in dialogue. Indeed, the very concepts of the interlocking circles, the five Cs, and the curricular weave give us a different language with which to articulate our own particular views and positions on educational reform. The Spanish and Portuguese Standards envision a seamless continuum in language education from K-16+. This all-inclusive structure presupposes an open and free dialogue among all of us.

In her recent book, *The Argument Culture: Moving from Debate to Dialogue*, Deborah Tannen decries the fact that our society sees every issue as a set of binary oppositional debates where one side must win at any cost. Moreover, Tannen emphasizes the myriad lost opportunities for productive dialogue when only the two extreme positions become salient in the argument, rather than many perspectives. June Phillips reminds us often that the content

Standards are at the heart of open communication about education reform today. Whether we embrace the Standards, reject them, or maintain an uncomfortable "wait and see" attitude toward them, it is imperative that we take advantage of them to engage in productive dialogue.

It is essential that we view articulation not merely as a K-12 versus post-secondary language curriculum issue, or as a language versus literature issue, or even as a language department versus language education department issue. The Standards speak to articulation between and among all levels and fields of the education continuum. We in post-secondary departments are part and parcel of this continuum. We are the ones who teach the future teachers, whether these are to be college or pre-college Spanish and/or Portuguese language and literature faculty. We are also the ones who teach the students who were taught by the pre-college faculty that populated our classes—our "grand-students." These grand-students may very well become the community leaders and politicians who will decide future curricular contexts. Or, in many cases, they may go on to become faculty themselves, teaching future teachers and community leaders, ad infinitum. Finally, we are the ones who need to be in the forefront of professional development K-16+.

In her recent *ACTFL White Paper*, Elizabeth Welles warns us that "the bulk of the faculty members [in higher education] who will encounter the high school graduates trained using the Standards are not yet informed about them." We need to add to this same bulk the future foreign language teachers who will be faced with Standards-based frameworks adopted by the states and who will not be well enough informed to handle the challenges that they will face. This gap in future teachers' education will persist if we, particularly those of us in language and literature departments, do not attempt to become better informed ourselves. Joan Kelly Hall poses an implicit incongruity between what future K-12 teachers need and what they get from language and literature departments, where Hall maintains that the faculty "rarely have background knowledge in theories and practices of foreign language learning" (49). She goes on to say, "until the curricula of all university language programs themselves are organized around the communication standards, the successful transformation of K-12 programs is likely to be problematic" (49). The implicit discontinuities cited by Hall point to the different cultural contexts that exist in many post-secondary settings. We can continue to wish that the Other would change or we can use our differences to foster dialogue. It is by our very differences reflected in our particular cultures that future K-16+ teachers may begin to experience "the weave" of language learning. It is in the diversity of cultures and communities that we will begin to make the connections and comparisons needed for fruitful communication.

During the work on the Spanish and Portuguese Standards, the task force began to grapple with issues of dialogue among the many cultures in our profession. It became clear to all of us that the Standards, as we envisioned them, could not be designed only for K-12, but needed to be thought through as a K-16+ project. When freshmen arrive at our institutions after having had a long sequence of the five Cs in one language, they will expect more from us. However, before we look for them to enter our classes, we need to be cognizant of those who are currently there and who will be their future teachers.

The Standards for Foreign Language Learning in general and the language specific Standards in particular provide us with a common language, a useful vocabulary, and an emerging common culture to allow us a better understanding of our individual roles and of our individual fields. We are coming into the acquisition of this new language—the language of the Standards, at several different entry points—much like our Spanish and Portuguese students in the K-16+ continuum. We propose that all 2, 707 post-secondary foreign language and literature departments in the country devise ways to become acquainted with this common language in our profession. Each individual department will have to decide the best way within its own context. Fundamental for this process is one of the tenets of the Standards—they are "student-centered." We, the college and university faculty are the students in question, and we have to understand and see the need and the importance of learning this new language domain.

The Standards are not a threat to the integrity of our fields of endeavor whether we pursue analyses of literary texts and other cultural aesthetic products, whether we pursue the analyses of second language acquisition and other cultural connections, or whether we pursue the analyses of teacher preparation and other cultural connections. The Standards give us a (pre)text, a common ground on which to map our interests and academic pursuits.

Whether we joined this conversation at its beginning, some six years ago, or whether we are just now joining it, we need to heed Dorothy James' *ACTFL White Paper* advice and "no longer slough [it] off as something that concerns someone else." James concludes that "we at the colleges need, with some humility, to inform ourselves about what is going on, and become a part of it." We emphasize here that this conversation is meant to be inclusive of all of us. If we choose not to participate, we will have only ourselves to blame in the future.

The task force that developed the Spanish and Portuguese Language Standards included members from the different cultures and different cultural contexts alluded to above. Ours was a three-year process during which we learned much about each other and each other's cultures. We clarified our own individual biases as well as our particular institutional circumstances. We have come a long way toward the realization articulated by Edward W. Said: "Underpinning the whole enterprise has to be some sense of history, not only as chronology but also the way Vico saw it, as actively made by human labor, of which the language-based humanities are a central part" (3). The process of internalizing the Standards—of learning the new language—has required time and patience and it is not complete even among us, the task-force members. We speak with many voices and from many viewpoints. Two of the contexts/positions represented in the task force belong to us, the authors of this chapter. One of us perceives herself as a "literature professor," primarily representing the traditional "content" department in a Ph.D. granting institution. The other of us perceives himself as a "language educator and administrator," primarily representing B.A. and M.A. granting institutions. Regardless of our academic "cultural background," we are all experiencing a period of transition that will certainly affect post-secondary education, 13-16+.

In an open letter to the presidents and chancellors of state universities and land-grant colleges in February, 1999, the Kellogg Commission on the Future of State and Land-Grant Universities concluded that "In the end, the clear evidence is that, with the resources and superbly qualified professors and staff on our campuses, we can organize our institutions to serve both local and national needs in a more coherent and effective way. We can and must do better" (i). The remainder of this third report by the Commission addresses the imperative for engagement, describes what it calls "the engaged university," and suggests what must be done in order to move from theory to actions.

The publication of the National Standards provides a point of departure for all post-secondary institutions to reflect on what might become a most desirable change in our attitudes toward teaching and learning languages, literatures, and cultures, and provides us with the opportunity to make the dramatic changes likely to be necessary if our curricula are going to accommodate the new language learner envisioned in the document. Because there will be at least a decade (and probably more) before these students reach our classes at the university level, there may be a tendency to diminish the need for substantive change in our curricula. However, we cannot look at the Standards as the only factor arguing for change in our departments.

In a recent volume providing multiple perspectives on research and scholarship in teaching languages, literatures, and culture, Heidi Byrnes ("Introduction") warns us of a number of factors combining to threaten the ecology of foreign languages departments in higher education. She cautions us that our "traditional humanistic engagement with literature is in danger of being carelessly thrown overboard when departments interpret student demand for a greater range of ways to become engaged with other cultures and language as a dismissal of literature as a way to know oneself and others" (10). She also calls for us to maintain our presence as an intellectually valid contributor within the academy by maintaining a balance between a broadened and intellectually stimulating curriculum and a service-oriented curriculum that exists primarily for the benefit of other programs and professional schools. Similarly, we must recognize that we are creating problems for ourselves when our scheduling practices create "serious faculty resource mismatches when senior and experienced faculty members, who typically are educated in a literary field, teach few students, while novice graduate TAs teach the bulk of students in language classes" (Byrnes 11).

Dorothy James (1997) managed to encapsulate the tunnel vision reality that is rather pervasive across departments of languages and literatures by describing her arrival at the University of London at the age of fifteen:

> The chair of the German department of Bedford College, an indomitable professor of the old school, Edna Purdie, called the new undergraduate students entering the department together and said, "For the next three years you will be devoting your time to German language and literature, not to the passing of examinations. By the end of three years, you will be able to read and understand anything written in the German language from the eighth century to the present day. That is your goal." None of us were particularly surprised to hear this. We *thought* that was why we were there. We had come to college to study German language and literature. My only complaint about Professor Purdie was that her "present day" stopped at about 1914 — all literature after that she considered too modern to view objectively, and thus not suitable for us. (43-44)

With great insight, James continues her discussion by pointing out that, although the experience she related occurred forty years ago, the systems currently in place in this country have "been largely modeled on systems appropriate to that kind of time and that kind of place. Our time and our place are different" (44).

It is this difference between the goals that most of us learned to expect as the driving forces in our own academic experience in languages and the proposed goals of the National Standards that underlies our greatest challenge to implementation of this new vision of language teaching and learning. We are, in effect, re-defining just what it means to know and be able to function effectively in a second or foreign language.

Pragmatically, our discussion should be limited to issues of curriculum at this point, since it serves no purpose to reflect on the formal preparation of the current professoriate. However, our recommendations and implementation plans must be informed by the scope of awareness of curriculum design and adaptability to change likely to be found among our colleagues. Whatever changes are to be made may infringe upon the "comfort zone" of many, but should not be perceived as a serious threat to academic stability and professional future. In other words, effective change will come only through collaboration. Efforts toward change will be stifled if attempted through confrontation. In addition, we must heed the issues mentioned above that Byrnes has highlighted. What then are the specific challenges that face us?

PH.D. GRANTING INSTITUTIONS

According to the Modern Language Association of America, 469 post-secondary foreign languages departments offer the Ph.D. degree in languages, literatures, linguistics, and/or second language acquisition. These departments, found in Colleges of Arts and Sciences or Colleges of Humanities, may be called Romance Languages, Modern Languages, or Spanish and Portuguese. In addition, Schools and Colleges of Education throughout the country offer doctoral degrees (Ph.D. and Ed.D.) in Foreign Language Pedagogy and Methodology. All of these departments account for the education of future post-secondary faculty, whether they end up in Ph.D. granting departments or in those that offer only the B.A. with or without the M.A. Although our discussion here may well apply to all doctoral-granting departments, we will focus primarily on those institutions where "content" and "methodology" are taught in two different departments if not in two different colleges. Historically, the departments to which we refer, with very few exceptions, are traditional departments of literature whose faculty members do not consider themselves to be in the business of K-12 teacher education (Tesser). Departments range from those having curricula that are fully integrated in languages, literatures, and cultures, attempting to form a seamless continuum from beginning courses to doctoral level seminars, to those dividing "language skills" from "literary analyses" through structural, physical and often hierarchical boundaries. Wherever the departments lie in the continuum, they do share some commonalties: enrollment pressures in Spanish classes; graduate teaching assistants; many tenured faculty members who are products of an education that valued individual work over collaborative endeavors; and the technology revolution.

Faculty in these departments perceive themselves as "over-worked," and the idea of further distancing themselves from their initial area of expertise—a particular period in literature or a particular issue in linguistics—is both threatening and overwhelming. Moreover, most Ph.D. granting institutions by definition are research universities; therefore, the emphasis for rewards is placed on "research publication" rather than on a conversation about perspectives, attitudes, and a new way of thinking about endeavors. One of the greatest challenges facing us at the end of this millennium is how to involve colleagues, young and old, in the productive dialogue that promises to change our profession

In the summer 1999 issue of the *ACTFL Newsletter*, Dale L. Lange, responding to Elizabeth Welles and Dorothy James, outlines four items that may be of help in addressing the incorporation of Standards in post-secondary settings. These are: 1) dissemination of the Standards and discussion of implications for post-secondary language programs, 2) articulation of programs (for continuous language learning K-16), 3) examination of assessment, and 4) placement from one level to another. In all cases, Lange points to the work of professional organizations and their journals, cooperative endeavors among organizations, and possibilities of future research. If we take these four items and combine them with the common elements among many Ph.D. granting departments, we may be able to offer an agenda for bringing our colleagues from traditional "content" departments into the conversation.

Although the technology of the printed page still requires us to present ideas in a sequential order, we need to think of these ideas in terms of the weave or of the interlocking circles found in the Standards: each idea depends on, builds on, and gives meaning to the other.

WORK THROUGH AND WITH PROFESSIONAL ORGANIZATIONS

Ph.D. granting departments of languages, literatures, and cultures depend on professional organizations and their refereed journals for credibility among other departments in the research university. Traditionally, PhD. granting departments have looked to the Modern Language Association for professionally accepted norms. It is usually at the MLA that these departments first interview prospective new faculty for their ranks; it is at the MLA that graduate students aspiring to teach in one of these departments look for mentoring.   Finally, it is through the Association of Departments of Foreign Languages, a division of the MLA, that the administrators of many of these departments engage in professional development.   While the AATSP and ACTFL are also represented among the ranks of the faculty in Ph.D. granting departments, it is not realistic to think that they have replaced the MLA in influence.

The MLA Executive Council endorsed the Standards, and MLA representatives consistently participate in Standards activities. Moreover, the MLA has publicly endorsed articulation K-16 through national projects and the publication of a collection of essays, *Preparing a Nation's Teachers* (Franklin, Laurence, and Welles). At its annual meeting, the MLA has added many sessions on pedagogy as well as specifically on the Standards.   Our emphasis on the MLA in this section is purposeful: colleagues in Ph.D. granting institutions will be more likely to discuss a new idea that carries MLA endorsement.   By working collaboratively through and with the MLA, we will be able to reach a greater number of colleagues.

GRADUATE TEACHING ASSISTANTS AND ENROLLMENT PRESSURES

Most Ph.D. granting departments have always made use of graduate teaching in lower division language courses. In this age of accountability, and as a result of many national treatises on the quality of undergraduate education, most Ph.D. granting departments now have required methods courses for teaching assistants. In the last two decades, many of these departments have made use of a Language Program Coordinator (LPC). In the most positive situations, this person is an applied linguist, an expert in second language acquisition, or a specialist in language education who is hired into the professorial ranks

We will not enter here into the discussion of the difficulty of this position. Suffice it to say that in many cases, the LPC came from a different culture (that of pedagogy or applied linguistics) and, therefore, suffered in departments where the majority of the faculty represented the culture of literary studies. The successful LPCs — those who were able to move through the ranks, obtain tenure and, in some cases, become department heads — were those who successfully engaged in cross-cultural communication. The successful LPCs in Ph.D. granting institutions are now in a position to influence the future generation of college faculty. In their interaction with graduate students, in their program development, and in their selection of textbooks, they can infuse the curriculum with the Standards.

Enrollment pressures in Spanish have forced departments to look for different ways to meet the demands of undergraduates. Many are hiring part-time and adjunct faculty to staff lower division classes. Graduate students are now teaching intermediate language courses as well as introductory courses in linguistics, literature, and culture/civilization. Some Ph.D. granting departments have also begun to offer courses on the teaching of literature. Those who are developing these courses clearly see a need for mentoring of young colleagues — graduate students — in pedagogical concerns. Moreover, the AATSP, MLA, and ACTFL have started offering more sessions at their annual meetings on the teaching of literature, thus bringing open conversation about issues of pedagogical concerns into the literary realm.

TENURED FACULTY

Although most literature faculty matured in the culture of individual work over collaborative work, most doctoral granting departments can point to curriculum development projects that by necessity have to involve many faculty. Ph.D. granting departments routinely conduct seminars presenting new ideas in the field and/or new research projects. The culture of those departments is one that encourages going to "lectures" by "innovative experts."

Social scientists have studied attitudes and influence for years. What we may learn from them is that we tend to give credibility to people "like us" but who do not "live with us." To reach the Ph.D. granting faculty, we will very likely need to make use of those who are most like them — primarily literary scholars — and who are also interested in the Standards movement. They are the ones that can exert the most powerful influence on colleagues.

USE OF TECHNOLOGY

Ph.D. granting departments have not been on the forefront of the technological revolution. However, some faculty members have ventured out to develop "technology infused" courses as well as web-based courses. Most departments have someone on the faculty who is interested in technology, and that person may be able to incorporate "Standards-thinking" into their own research and teaching, if they are asked to enter into the conversation.

Those of us who have been involved in the development of the language-specific Standards, and who have followed the progress of this movement in the last few years, have seen the impact that the document has had in curriculum development in K-12 schools throughout the country. Moreover, we have seen accrediting organizations and assessment organizations go to Standards-based programs. We have also seen, for the first time this century, professional organizations representing the different cultures of our fields sitting together and engaging in open conversation about the implications of the Standards.

The Ph.D. granting department will not be the first to enter the conversation. Furthermore, these departments will not enter it peacefully. Many colleagues in these departments are not interested and do not want to be bothered by any process that will change the way things are done. In our effort to reform curricula and to begin a new way of thinking about what we do, we cannot afford to allow the Ph.D. granting department to distance itself from the Standards. These are the departments that are educating a large majority of post-secondary faculty members, and until they are involved, indeed until they are invested in the dialogue, change will be slower than we wish.

B.A. AND M.A. GRANTING DEPARTMENTS

The perspective from the B.A./M.A. granting department may be a bit different from that of a doctoral degree institution. One of the authors of this essay is chairperson of such a department at a major land-grant institution. The pressures and conditions in these departments present other challenges within the picture that we have addressed up to this point. All language departments, but very specifically B.A. and M.A. granting institutions, must respond to five new imperatives if programs and curricula are to be driven by the Standards. Although the following recommendations reflect changes that can be made at institutions offering Bachelor's and

Master's degrees, they may be appropriate for Ph.D. granting institutions as well.

FOCUS GOALS ON PROCESS

Rhetoric in vogue needs to be based less in terms of product, and more in terms of process. We need to refocus our course goals, indeed our curricular goals, to think less in terms of a "final paper with all the bells and whistles" presented at the end of the particular course or curriculum, and more in terms of the steps in the development of that final product. It is imperative that we focus on the process of education and remind central administrators that we are not a business whose products, college graduates, are fully "finished" at graduation. Instruction at all levels should be designed to guide the development of critical thinking skills — hypothesizing, supporting opinion, divergent thinking — more than to direct the preparation of a final paper, or the parroting back of factual data already contained in the textbooks and in the professors' yellowed notes.

TEACH CULTURE INTERACTIVELY

All faculty should take a more interactive approach to the teaching of culture. Our goal should be to heighten our students' awareness of culture "universals," and to develop strategies for recognizing and defining cultures through comparisons of both common and unique characteristics of these universals. That is, we need to focus our goals on those issues that define us as human beings — family, rituals, rites of passage, definitions of success — that exist in all cultures but may be manifested in different ways. The courses in our departments can be designed so that students engage in cultural as well as linguistic comparisons and connections. Courses in language, linguistics, literature, and culture remain at the heart of our programs. These are the courses that our faculties are best qualified to teach, and indeed are most interested in teaching. To engage our colleagues in "Standards" conversation, those of us who are committed to the objectives outlined in the Five Cs should look for connections between this newly developing culture in our field and that of our current colleagues. If we believe that the change is necessary, it is incumbent upon us to engage in successful cross-cultural communication with our colleagues. It is in this context that we can help our colleagues and our students attain the goals set forth in the Standards.

EMPHASIZE INFORMATION ACCESS

All of our departments should help students learn to access and use the information available to them through a range of media. Many students are quite versed in computer skills, internet navigation, and interactive computing facilities. Those of us in B.A. and M.A. granting departments need to guide our students toward the possibilities of using their skills to find information that will benefit their study of foreign languages and cultures. Once the information is collected, students need to know how to organize the data and how to process these data so that they are meaningful within the frame of reference to which they apply. In their quest for information, students will need guidance in identifying point of view, hidden ideological positions, and ambiguity. This will require us to guide students as they strive to grasp information, concepts, and ideas, and diminish the quest for transliteration from one linguistic code to another, or transposition of an idea to their own cultural point of view without questioning the validity of such exercise. In other words, as we encourage more technological exploration on the part of our students, we need to design our courses so that they become increasingly critical and analytical thinkers who are able to process information through something other than their own original cultural and linguistic templates. This, in its most basic form, is the goal of the entire educational process. At the same time, we must remain cognizant of the possibility that some content and skill development areas are not necessarily best served by technology. As important as the ability to find data is the ability to interpret it, and this often may be done most effectively and efficiently in the conventional classroom, rather than in the electronic classroom. At the same time, web-based delivery of instruction may enable us to move these interactive real-time discussions beyond the four walls of the classroom and involve a much more geographically disparate group in our discussions.

TEACH LANGUAGE IN MULTIPLE CONTEXTS

Throughout our programs, we should place greater emphasis on the appropriateness of Spanish and Portuguese languages to different contexts. Opportunities for students to become directly involved in informal discussion on topics of interest to them, as well as opportunities to present organized papers in a more formal setting, need to be included in all courses. By encouraging and supporting the professional involvement of our students even at the undergraduate level, we instill in them an awareness of the existence of a network of people who share their interests, and help them begin to develop their self-images as proficient and respected users of Spanish and/or Portuguese.

MOVE LANGUAGE BEYOND THE CLASSROOM

We need to move language and culture beyond the classroom. No longer can we remain satisfied with the ability of our students simply to "survive" in the host culture. Our challenge is to endow them with the linguistic skills and knowledge that will make it possible for them to become full participatory members of the language community. In most cultures, this requires that they have an advanced level of proficiency in the oral and written language, and that their behavior be governed by the "must-dos and taboos" of the culture. They should have an awareness of the geographical and historical hallmarks of the countries, and enough knowledge of the music, art, architecture, literature, and scientific accomplishments (i.e., the Culture) that represent and define the host group to be able to discuss these topics informally. While much of the content of our courses covers these areas, we have not necessarily "operationalized" our students' awareness of them beyond responses to items on a test. Even in our literature classes, we focus on critical analysis of the canon, largely ignoring the popular literature of the country. So, while a student might be able to speak eloquently about the Quixote, he or she would have absolutely nothing to say about the work of Pérez Reverte or some of the contemporary *ficción policíaca* so popular in Spain today.

In summary, we must re-evaluate the content of our curriculum in view of the Standards to provide the appropriate education for future k-12 teachers as well as to anticipate the changing needs of students who come into our courses with twelve or more years of foreign language study. Is the context of our curriculum adequate? Are our expectations of linguistic ability appropriate for the entry levels we are likely to find among our students? Do our courses build on what students already know and are able to do, or do we simply present them with more of the same? The answers to all of these questions pose the challenge to the post-secondary curriculum. The most obvious question that arises—for which there is not one best answer—is "how do we do that?" The key, however, will lie in the ability to provide dynamic, persistent, and persuasive leadership to departments as they confront and respond to these imperatives.

To this point, we have posed more questions than we have provided answers. What follows is a suggested plan of action.

Although this plan is still a "suggestion" for change, a similar plan is currently being followed in the M.A. granting departmental unit of one of the authors. The results of this on-going process will not become apparent for years to come. We stated at the beginning of this chapter that our primary goal is to engage as many of our colleagues as possible in a process that is changing the way we will conduct our business of "teaching, serving, and inquiring into the nature of things." We reaffirm that statement here and add that this is a dynamic process that will continue to evolve as we become more conversant on its topics. It is imperative that we allow the process to evolve, lest we fall into the trap of change for change's sake. The change proposed here is one that will bring about healthy questioning of our disciplinary and cultural positions. In so doing, we will sharpen our own critical thinking skills and thereby will become better teachers to our students.

DEVELOPING A PLAN OF ACTION

If departments of languages, literatures, and cultures at post-secondary institutions are to implement substantive change, the first thing that they must do is begin to think "outside the box." To do so, however, we must first accept the fact that there is a "box." This, in turn, will necessitate our colleagues' and our own willing-ness to leave egos at the door as we embark upon the challenges associated with redesigning curricula. The most critical aspect of the process that is described below is the shift in the focus of the thinking of the faculty so that it becomes student-centered instead of self (faculty) centered. Conceptually, the questions are designed to have faculty first hypothesize an ideal curriculum, then look at the strengths and limitations of the students, and finally to speculate on what students are likely to need to know and be able to do once they graduate from the program. Finally, faculty are asked to evaluate the current departmental program in light of the new focus on the students.

In order to begin on common ground, a clear definition of curriculum should be established. One effective definition refers to curriculum as the establishment of

> a sequence of educational opportunities for learners that builds on internal interrelations and continuities among the major units of instruction (at the college level, a course is the traditional unit) to enhance learning. Critical considerations are the selection of content and its sequencing — the what of the curriculum — and its delivery in

both the larger educational environment and the particular
instructional setting — the how of the curriculum."

(Byrnes, "Constructing Curricula" 265)

Faculty should be reminded that there is the concept of
Curriculum by default, which is "a curriculum whose primary
intellectual motivation and force reside at the level of the
individual course, which is taught by a single faculty member and
evaluated by students as a separate and independent entity"
(Byrnes 269). There is also the idea of **Curriculum by design**,
which is a program in which "all teaching faculty members of a
department engage deliberately in building a consensus about
what constitutes knowledge in the foreign language field, about
what the large educational outcomes should be, and about how
individual courses can provide interrelated avenues for students to
gain that knowledge" (270). The goal of the entire initiative is to
pursue activities that will result in a curriculum by design, rather
than by default.

One question that can be posed to initiate and encourage
divergent thinking is "If there were no limits to our resources and
capabilities, what would we identify as the essential skills
necessary for a graduate to possess at the end of the sequence of
undergraduate study? At the end of the sequence of graduate
study?" This works best in a retreat or seminar setting, where an
entire day (or more) can be dedicated to the issues to be discussed,
without the distractions of answering telephones, checking e-mail,
teaching classes, etc.

In preparation for the day's activities, a sufficient quantity of
newsprint pads and broad felt-tip markers should be distributed
among the groups of participants. A maximum of five members
per group works well; the odd number discourages pairings within
the group. In the small groups, faculty can begin to generate group
lists of essential skills and areas of knowledge for undergraduates
and graduates, writing their lists on the newsprint and posting
them on the walls of the room for presentation to and discussion by
the larger group. At the end of the retreat, all posters should be
transcribed to diskette for future use during the curriculum
development initiative.

The second session, which includes reconstituted faculty
working groups, can respond to the following questions: Do our
expectations of our students limit their possibilities to succeed?
How well do we know our students? To what extent does our
"awareness" of their limitations become a self-fulfilling prophecy?
What are reasonable expectations? How do we express these
expectations? How do we communicate them to students? Do our

promotional materials, course syllabi, reading lists, etc., reflect these expectations? Do we really have truth in advertising with respect to our programs? Again, following a period of group discussion, ideas should be written on newsprint and posted around the room, where each group presents its responses to the other participants. These two sessions will probably occupy about one and one-half hours each.

As the emphasis becomes more and more centered on student needs, the working groups can be challenged to consider what their program would look like ten years from now if there were no limits to resources and capabilities. What would be the profiles of the graduate and undergraduate programs? What would it be that sets these programs apart from all of the other programs in the country? What would attract students to this institution instead of to peer institutions? How might the faculty begin to relate the discipline more closely with other units in the College? Outside the College? Why should students pursue the study of a foreign language? What will the department have to offer to the student whose primary purpose in obtaining a degree is to be gainfully employed upon graduation? Following the established format, these questions should be discussed first in groups and then with the participants as a whole.

At this point, it would be appropriate to begin to address the issue of curriculum planning, keeping in mind that the task facing the group is not to oppose change, but to control it. They can now be asked to begin to formulate goals that the unit can set with respect to total enrollments, numbers of majors, breadth of the curriculum, preparation of students, the incorporation of technology into instruction, their own professional development, and their own personal achievement. Faculty should be encouraged to focus on possibilities, rather than on limitations or constraints.

The next step would be to begin to address ways in which faculty might realize the goals, once they are established. Questions to be posed could include: What support does the unit need to realize their vision? What needs to be done that might not require external support? What initiatives might be grant supported? Consideration should be given to such things here as the development of new courses, articulation (both horizontal and vertical), scheduling, syllabus design, and assessment. Does the department need to have a threshold examination for entry into a major area of study? Should there be an exit examination for graduation? If so, who designs and administers these assessments?

How will the department assess its progress and performance? What incentives could be offered to make the effort worthwhile?

Once a large list of goals has been compiled, the group should then prioritize the list of what is to be accomplished as a result of the curricular initiative upon which the unit is embarking. Finally, a time frame should be established and a plan of action should be drafted. This may necessitate modifying the traditional departmental approaches to faculty meetings, and might even impact upon existing governance and committee structures. Specifically, the group must identify the tasks to be carried out and determine the ways in which they will be completed. Does the unit want to work with the existing committee structures, or re-configure them? Should the entire faculty meet regularly in working sessions to accomplish their tasks, or work individually in small groups? What kinds of support will the group need in order to complete the program revision by the desired date?

It should be noted that the unit is likely to be working on the establishment and attainment of goals at two levels: goals and a plan of action for improvement of the unit, and goals and a plan of action that address what students know and are able to do at the end of their sequence of instruction. With respect to the curricular initiative, the course and program revision is subsumed under the larger initiative to improve the overall effectiveness of the department and to attain the vision the group has for the unit.

ACTIVITIES FOLLOWING THE RETREAT

Obviously, a one or two-day retreat does not provide enough time for a faculty to restructure its curriculum. Viewed more broadly, the entire process would likely follow a sequence that includes:
   Establishment of a Departmental Vision
   Establishment of a Departmental Mission Statement
   Development of Departmental Goals (Student Outcome
      Statements)
   Development of a Departmental Core Program of Study (generic)
   Development of Content-specific Programs of Study
   Review of Current Courses, and Additions, Modifications, and
      Deletions
   Establishment of Comprehensive Formative and Summative
      Program Assessment Procedures
   Establishment of a Mechanism for Continuing Program Revision

It would not be unreasonable to expect that faculty would need to meet on a regular basis, perhaps as frequently as once every two weeks, in order to accomplish this revision. It is also imperative that administrators at the college and central administrative levels be aware of and supportive of the initiative, since the changes are likely to have far-reaching effects in terms of faculty work load, future staffing decisions, etc.

Each called meeting of the faculty should have a specific goal to accomplish. Although there will be considerable interest on the part of some faculty members to move immediately to a discussion of courses that should be added, modified, and/or deleted, the meeting facilitator must be insistent that the tasks leading up to course design and revision be completed before moving into that phase of curriculum development. Following the establishment of departmental goals, content-specific groups will need to particularize these goals to the appropriate areas of concentration (e.g., Linguistics, Portuguese, Spanish). Once that is done, each course listed in the catalog should be reviewed to see that it makes a direct and substantive contribution to the attainment of the stated goals.

CONCLUSION

We began this chapter by setting the stage at the post-secondary level. By allowing representative voices from the profession to speak, we presented the state of the "conversation" at this point in the development of the Standards project. Our review of the process as it stands now indicates slow progress among post-secondary faculty. We then presented issues and challenges for the Ph.D. granting institutions, and finally we posed the view from B.A. and M.A. granting institutions. Our goal was to take the reader from the general view of post-secondary Spanish and Portuguese education through the process through which many of us have gone: from a general conversation to a reality check on the education of future post-secondary faculty, to specific ideas and challenges facing the undergraduate curriculum.

Redesigning curriculum is never easy. At the university level, it has been compared in difficulty to attempting to move a graveyard, which may be a very appropriate analogy. In view of the widespread impact the Standards are likely to have, however, failure to respond to the opportunity to revise the programs we offer at the post-secondary level could well result in departments becoming graveyards, should they refuse to move in the direction necessary to meet the needs of a new generation of students.

WORKS CITED

Byrnes, Heidi. "Introduction." *Learning Foreign and Second Languages.* Ed. Heidi Byrnes. New York: Modern Language Association, 1998. 1-22.

_____. "Constructing Curricula in Foreign Language Departments." *Learning Foreign and Second Languages*. Ed. Heidi Byrnes. New York:MLA, 1998. 262-95.

Franklin, Phyllis, David Laurence, and Elizabeth B. Welles, eds. *Preparing a Nation's Teachers: Models for English and Foreign Language Programs*. New York: MLA, 1999.

Hall, Joan Kelly. "The Communication Standards." *Foreign Language Standards: Linking Research, Theories, and Practices*. Eds. June K. Phillips and Robert M. Terry. Chicago: National Textbook Co., 1999. 15-66.

James, Dorothy. "Bypassing the Traditional Leadership: Who's Minding the Store?" *Profession 1997*. Ed. Phyllis Franklin. New York: Modern Language Association, 1997. 41-53.

_____. "The Impact on Highter Education of Standards for Foreign Language Learning: Preparing for the 21st Century." *ACTFL White Paper*. *ACTFL Newsletter* 11.1 (1998): 11-14.

Kellogg Commission on the Future of State and Land-Grant Universities. *Returning to our Roots: The Engaged Institution*. Washington, D.C.: National Association of State Universities and Land-Grant Colleges, 1999.

Krashen, Stephen D. *Foreign Language Education: The Easy Way*. Culver City, California, 1997.

Lange, Dale L. "Response to the Welles and James Articles." *ACTFL Newsletter* 11.4 (1999): 9-11

Marks, Elaine. "Loving Words: Nightmares and Pleasures of a Glossophile; or The Advocacy of Semiotic Bliss." *MIFLC Review*. 7 (1997-98): 11-19.

Phillips, June K., and Jamie B. Draper. *The Five Cs: The Standards for Foreign Language Learning Work Text*. New York: Heinle & Heinle, 1999.

Said, Edward W. "An Unresolved Paradox." *MLA Newsletter* 31 (1999): 3.

Swaffar, Janet. "Major Changes: The Standards Project and the New Foreign Language Curriculum." *ADFL Bulletin* 30.1 (1998): 34-7.

Tannen, Deborah. The Argument Culture: Moving from Debate to Dialogue. New York: Random House, 1998.

Tesser, Carmen Chaves. "Who We Are and How They See Us: On Shaping an Image through the Other's Perception." *ADFL Bulletin* 30.2 (1999): 6-9.

VanPatten, Bill. "What is Second Language Acquisition and What is it Doing in this Department?" *ADFL Bulletin* 30.3 (1999): 49-53.

Welles, Elizabeth. "Standards for Foreign Language Learning: Implications and Perceptions." *ACTFL White Paper*. *ACTFL Newsletter* 11 (1998): 7-9.

8

FACTORS THAT AFFECT THE IMPLEMENTATION OF THE STANDARDS

Martha Singer Semmer
Chair, AATSP Public Advocacy Committee

Language and communication are at the heart of the human experience. The United States must educate students who are equipped linguistically and culturally to communicate successfully in a pluralistic American society and abroad. This imperative envisions a future in which ALL students will develop and maintain proficiency in English and at least one other language, modern or classical.

(National Standards in Foreign Language Education Project 1999, 7)

The importance of Spanish in the world and the growing presence of Spanish speakers and Hispanic cultures in the United States have, in large part, inspired the visionary spirit of this document. In contrast to the vision of long, articulated sequences of instruction expressed here, however, the reality of Spanish education in the United States today is quite different. (438)

Responsibilities of foreign language education professionals include the obligation to ensure that all students of all ages have access to foreign language study as an integral component of the core academic curriculum; and that all students of all ages should have the opportunity—through a long-sequence program of high-quality instruction—to achieve the standards, thus achieving high proficiency in foreign language(s).

Currently, in many places a tremendous gap exists between the vision of the implementation of standards and the reality of language programs. Although scattered model programs do exist in which the "vision" and the "reality" are united as one, the majority of Spanish language education programs lies somewhere between the two. It is critical that factors positively affecting the implementation of standards be nurtured and that those that are negative be molded and shaped into positive factors. If foreign language educators do not lead towards the "vision" of the implementation of standards, no one else will.

Many existing factors influence change. This chapter begins with the focus on the student (referring to all students) and then spirals outward to include teachers of Spanish, foreign language teachers in general, school personnel and institutions, and professional language and related organizations or associations. Beyond the education arena, this chapter also addresses parents; decision makers/policymakers at the local, state and national levels; and to some extent, the international or world community. The order in which the factors are treated in no way represents an order of importance, except that the student always occupies first place. A section on program planning and implementing the standards will bring this chapter to a close.

LANGUAGE LEARNING FOR ALL STUDENTS

Some prevalent myths about language learning for all students must be dispelled before language learning programs will become accessible to all students as part of the core academic curriculum. Such misconceptions include the following:

- My child doesn't even know English and they're trying to teach him/her a foreign language.
- You have to be smart to learn another language.
- Foreign language study is not for everyone, just for those going to college. And besides, students only need two years to get into most colleges.
- Students with learning disabilities or those identified for Special Education are incapable of learning a foreign language.
- If one cannot learn a language in two years, one does not have a knack for learning a foreign language.

Students do not believe these myths unless they are conditioned to believe them. However, once students do come to believe such negative tenets about themselves, they form an embedded low self-esteem regarding their abilities to learn a foreign language. In addition, children are often conditioned to believe the following:

- Children whose heritage language is Spanish should be learning English, not Spanish. After all, they already know Spanish.
- Children whose home language is a language other than English or Spanish should learn English, not a third language.

- When students study Spanish or another language, it takes away from their academic progress in other content areas.
- There is no need to learn a foreign language. After all, the whole world speaks English.

All the above statements negatively affect the implementation of standards. The "vision" of *Standards for Learning Spanish* (National Standards...Project 1999, 431-74) will not come to fruition for all students without changing negative beliefs about students and how students themselves perceive their abilities regarding language learning. The other major factor is that only a low percentage of students — without some form of accelerated learning, such as living for an extensive period of time in a Hispanic culture — can achieve the standards and reach high proficiency levels, if they start at the middle school, high school or post-secondary level. All students can learn Spanish or other languages if they start early enough and if they have high-quality instruction.

The achievement of the standards through long-sequence Spanish education programs will happen if the K-12 curriculum is based on the following belief statements:

- The study of a foreign language enhances English proficiency and English literacy while developing proficiency in the foreign language (Marcos).
- If you can speak one language, you can learn to speak more than one language. Furthermore, brain research indicates the importance of learning more than one language at an early age (Begley).
- Foreign language study has been identified as an important subject for K-12 students in the National Educational Goals and a number of state academic frameworks (Boston).
- Students with disabilities can experience success with Spanish or another language (Marcos). Nevertheless, teaching students with disabilities requires that teachers use different teaching strategies, have realistic expectations, and assess progress consistent with the adapted goals, not necessarily the goals and expectations of the majority of the class (Shrum and Glisan).
- All students can learn a language if given enough time with the language and adequate instruction. (Curtain & Pesola; National Standards...Project 1999, 19).

- All children should be encouraged to become proficient and literate in their heritage language. Simultaneous development of the heritage language and English helps these children become more proficient in both languages (De Houwer). Also, they learn that their language and culture are valued and respected, resulting in high self-esteem.
- From personal experience, this writer, like many other teachers, finds that students who study Spanish or another language as a third or fourth language learn language more quickly and they also progress well as they learn English.
- Students who study a foreign language generally outperform students who do not study a foreign language on tests of basic skills. (Rafferty, as cited in Marcos). In addition, students who are involved in sound FLES programs appear to outperform monolingual peers in metacognitive and cognitive processing. (Robinson).
- Local, state, national and international businesses and agencies are realizing the importance and the benefits to their companies as they hire employees who are proficient in Spanish and/or other languages (Voght & Uber Grosse).

These statements about language learning must constantly remain in the foreground in order to plan, implement, and maintain K-16 language programs.

DIVERSE LEARNERS

For decades language study has been considered to be valuable for select groups of students and usually at the secondary level. Those going on to college have often taken a minimum of two years of a foreign language in order to be admitted to a college or university. In a number of schools, junior high language programs were established for academic students, eventually followed by middle school programs, which have typically been "exploratory." In exploratory programs, after experiencing two or more foreign languages for up to a full year, middle school students decide which language they want to continue into high school. Traditionally, this scenario has been the major source of foreign language students.

Fortunately, the national and state standards movements are changing the belief system of many people regarding who should undertake the study of a foreign language. Foreign language professionals have led the movement in establishing a guiding principle that language learning is an academic subject for all students. The only way the majority of students can reach the necessary proficiency levels of the identified standards is to begin language study in the early years of school, such as in kindergarten or pre-school. This vision has posed challenges for the foreign language education profession at each level of K-16 education. No longer do students in foreign language classes fit a singular description of the academic, college-bound, above-average, motivated students. If foreign language teachers are to meet the needs of all students, as they are obligated to do, it follows that teachers must be prepared and willing to teach diverse students.

Diverse students include students with special needs, students with learning disabilities, Limited English Proficient (LEP) students, students whose home language is not English, and students labeled as cognitively gifted and talented. Those with sight, speech and/or hearing problems or physical challenges require additional considerations. Diverse students in terms of social development may include those who exhibit severe behavior problems, often taking medication to control their behavior; students from dysfunctional families; and students with a different sexual orientation.

Diversity in the foreign language classroom actually reflects rich resources, which can strengthen and enhance foreign language learning for the entire class. The foreign language teacher is responsible for instilling in students the ethic of valuing and respecting diverse languages and cultures. How the foreign language teacher addresses diversity in the classroom forms a model for students regarding diversity in general. Undoubtedly, diversity poses challenges. It is important for the foreign language teacher to consult other school professionals such as counselors, speech therapists, physical therapists, and classroom teachers regarding students with special needs. Usually the most insightful persons to consult are the parents.

In closing this section, it is significant to note that society's negative perception of learning a foreign language often impacts the learner's frame of mind upon entering the foreign language class. What may at first appear to be a problem regarding the student's ability to learn, which in turn affects his or her success at achieving the standards, may actually be low self-esteem concerning language learning. There will be situations in which standards may need to be adapted to individual learners. Nevertheless, foreign language educators must develop eclectic teaching methods in order to address differentiated learning—that is, to teach to the Multiple Intelligences, different learning styles, and the unique characteristics of their students.

THE TEACHER'S ROLE

Foreign language teachers, including Spanish teachers, play the most significant roles regarding the successful implementation of the standards identified and explained in *Standards for Foreign Language Learning in the 21st Century* (National Standards... Project 1999) and particularly *Standards for Learning Spanish* (431-474). Foreign language teachers in general will have to demonstrate the following competencies and characteristics:

- High proficiency in the language(s) and culture(s) taught
- A thorough understanding of language acquisition theories and strategies as applied to the instruction of students of all ages in grades K-16
- Complete understanding of the standards and the ability to help students progress towards achieving them
- Willingness and ability to adapt teaching and the instructional program to reflect individual differences and capabilities as well as varied rates of learning
- Eagerness to adapt teaching and the instructional program to meet the needs of students who take advantage of longer sequences of instruction than in the past
- Enthusiasm to participate in foreign language professional organizations and professional development activities
- Desire to discuss and share foreign language teaching ideas
- Ability to collaborate with colleagues from different levels in order to provide students with a well-articulated, long-sequence program of instruction
- Zeal to advocate for foreign language study as part of the core academic curriculum
- Active participation in the community at large and non-foreign language professional organizations, such as a local education association in order to build coalitions that support foreign language education

Foreign language educators who maintain their language skills, remain current with respect to foreign language pedagogy, and keep abreast of issues and trends pertaining to foreign language education are invaluable to the successful implementation of standards. They understand the importance of careful articulation and qualified foreign language teachers at all levels, including the elementary school. Foreign language teachers who become involved in other education-related school and community activities garner additional support for foreign language education in general.

Spanish teachers find themselves in unique situations in that Spanish enrollments have increased significantly in comparison to other foreign language enrollments. Unfortunately, quantity does not automatically translate to quality of instructional programs; as enrollment increases, qualified teachers are in shorter supply and marginally-qualified teachers are expected to deliver programs that often fall short of providing the necessary learning situations for students to adequately achieve the standards.

THE EDUCATION SYSTEM

In education systems in which standards are most successfully implemented, foreign language education is an integral component of the academic curriculum. This means children experience high-quality foreign language instruction during the school day starting in kindergarten (even pre-school) and continuing through elementary school, middle school, high school, and college. Only qualified foreign language teachers are hired to teach, and these teachers are treated equitably with other teachers in professional education positions. Building and district support staff, teachers, principals, administrators, and other personnel all consider foreign languages to be a core academic subject. This is the scenario in which foreign language education ideally takes place.

However, most foreign language educators find themselves in less than ideal teaching situations. A closer examination of many programs of Foreign Language in the Elementary School (FLES) finds that the FLES teacher may not have adequate work space, may have a large number of students in a single class and a total student load of hundreds of students, and may teach in multiple buildings with inadequate travel time and inadequate compensation for travel time. Supervisors often expect children to achieve the goals of a long-sequence program, when in reality, children do not have enough instructional time to achieve those goals. Other unacceptable learning situations include an unqualified FLES teacher, a classroom teacher who is unqualified to teach FLES, or even an advanced high school student or an interested parent or volunteer teaching FLES. Sometimes FLES programs are offered only before or after school. These negatives can be turned into more workable situations over time, but not overnight. Most supervisors and administrators will listen to a rationale for changes in working conditions that will positively affect students. The issue of a school not using qualified FLES teachers or of a FLES program that is not valued enough to be offered as part of the regular elementary school curriculum can also be turned into a positive. If it is made clear that these are pilot programs or temporary steps to creating a FLES program that will be offered during the academic school day, then these situations are valuable building blocks to the development of a solid, long-sequence program.

Again, the ideal situation is that fifth or sixth graders enter a middle school program that builds on the elementary school experience. Middle school administrators do not always understand that a change is necessary in the foreign language program to accommodate incoming students, since most middle school programs have traditionally offered exploratory foreign language courses or no foreign language at all. Unfortunately, a number of middle school foreign language teachers also feel that a change in the program is unnecessary. As Protase Woodford has commented, "It [foreign language study] is something that takes place over time. The FLES program is essential. If you begin with something good, you'd better be sure that you've got continuity — that those kids are not dropped and then have to begin again. We talk about motivation. Think of how motivating it is to begin a language in grade one and then to have to begin a language in grade three and then all of a sudden to begin again in grade seven . . . and then to begin again in grade nine. That would de-motivate a saint." Many times students lose interest and drop language study at middle school because there is no program for them in which their language skills can continue to develop. The K-12 foreign language teachers need to collaborate, not only among themselves but also with other school and district personnel, to develop a well-articulated K-12 program. Also, students who have had a good FLES program are often ready and wanting to try another foreign language.

In recent years, articulation efforts between middle schools and high schools have allowed students to enter a foreign language class in high school at a more advanced level if they have successfully completed a specified number of years in the middle school. A district's K-12 foreign language teachers need to be involved in the planning of changes that also need to occur at the high school level. Once again, careful articulation is needed if students are to achieve the standards at a high proficiency level.

Post-secondary institutions also need to be ready for change. First and foremost, higher foreign language entrance requirements should be established. College entrance requirements dramatically affect the K-12 curriculum. Few colleges and universities require more than two years of a foreign language for entrance. Some colleges and universities do not require any foreign language coursework in order for students to be admitted.

Community colleges and four-year colleges and universities are also being challenged to change traditional foreign language programs. The recently developed post-secondary foreign language standards, which are included in the *Standards for Foreign Language Learning in the 21st Century* (National Standards...Project 1999), should be the guide to creating an improved college language curriculum. Of course, it is necessary to keep in mind that the visionary language-specific standards at the 13-16 level are based on twelve years of previous language study. As K-12 schools gradually change in order to offer language programs that allow students to achieve the grade-level foreign language standards, colleges and universities are going to experience greater fluctuations in proficiency levels. Higher education must plan and implement foreign language programs that take incoming students at uneven proficiency levels and provide instruction that leads to achievement of the standards. Many traditional foreign language programs at the post-secondary level will fall short of preparing students for the challenges of communicating successfully in a multilingual world. Post-secondary programs must be changed to better prepare students to achieve the standards of "what students should know and be able to do" in a global marketplace, in the multi-faceted professional world, as well as within multilingual and multicultural communities.

Colleges and universities that prepare foreign language teachers will need to re-evaluate their preparation programs. Teaching in foreign language programs that expect students to function at high proficiency levels in the 5 C's of Communication, Cultures, Connections, Comparisons, and Communities requires that foreign language teachers entering the schools of today and tomorrow be better prepared than ever before. In light of GOALS 2000 and state academic standards, colleges and universities also have an obligation to prepare all educators, including principals, classroom teachers, and counselors to understand the importance of long-sequence foreign language programs.

The implementation of K-16 foreign language standards will be granted the necessary support from the overall education system, only when the entire education system recognizes K-16 foreign language education as an academic subject within the core curriculum.

PROFESSIONAL ORGANIZATIONS

Professional foreign language organizations, such as the American Association of Teachers of Spanish and Portuguese (AATSP) and the American Council on the Teaching of Foreign Languages (ACTFL), are key to foreign language educators' continued professional growth. For many foreign language teachers, they serve as the primary source of professional development. State, regional, and national foreign language associations not only have responded to significant issues regarding K-16 foreign language education, but also have taken the lead in shaping it. Foreign language professionals at all levels of education should actively participate in professional associations, which allow teachers the guidance and support they need in order to implement standards.

Other local, state, and national professional and/or community organizations also affect the implementation of standards. Since foreign language education has not traditionally been considered an integral component of the core curriculum, foreign language professionals are obligated to educate organizations—such as parent teacher organizations, teacher education associations, school executive associations, and boards of education associations—about standards and the role of standards in K-16 foreign language education. Failure of non-foreign language professional organizations to value the vision of the standards will severely slow progress towards their implementation.

NATIONAL BOARD CERTIFICATION

Standards for accomplished foreign language teachers have been developed by the National Board for Professional Teaching Standards (NBPTS) Foreign Language Standards Committee with the belief that it is the professional duty of accomplished foreign language teachers to guide and help students achieve the student standards to a high level of proficiency. National Board Certified teachers will strengthen the foreign language profession; more importantly, they will demonstrate the teaching attributes and skills that are key to students' attaining high levels of proficiency for the implementation of standards. National Board Certified Foreign Language Teachers will demonstrate, through a standards-based assessment, their ability to address successfully the teacher standards detailed under the following section titles:

I.   Knowledge of Students
II.   Fairness
III.   Knowledge of Language
IV.   Knowledge of Culture
V.   Knowledge of Language Acquisition
VI.   Multiple Paths to Learning
VII.   Articulation of Curriculum and Instruction
VIII.   Learning Environment
IX.   Instructional Resources
X.   Assessment
XI.   Reflection and Professional Growth
XII.   Schools, Families, and Communities
XIII.   Professional Community
XIV.   Advocacy for Foreign Language Education
                                (Olkin)

The successful completion of the National Board Certification process should be a goal of every teacher as s/he moves along the career path. Because of a rigorous and comprehensive assessment process involving both a school-site portfolio and a day-long series of exercises in an assessment center, National Board Certification acknowledges the high competency level of each successful candidate. The standards document offers teachers an excellent set of guidelines that can be utilized as a professional development tool. Furthermore, the process of National Board Certification, which requires teachers to engage in reflection and analysis, offers teachers a valuable professional development experience, whether or not one achieves certification. Note that scores are "banked" for up to three years so that candidates can retake portions of the assessment.

Local school districts and states often provide incentives for teachers to become National Board Certified. Information regarding National Board Certification can be obtained from local school districts, state departments of education, and the National Board for Professional Teaching Standards web site at http://www.nbpts.org/ .

PARENTS

The majority of adult Americans never had the opportunity to become proficient in a language other than English, even though they may have studied a language for at least two years in high school. They wonder why they can't speak the language. Many adults had negative experiences with learning a foreign language, and since they believe that they never needed to know one, many parents do not understand the significance of their children becoming proficient in at least one language besides English. Obviously, such attitudes negatively affect the implementation of the standards.

On the other hand, parents who have experienced foreign language learning at an early age, or who are proficient in a foreign language, thoroughly understand the importance of their children beginning an academic program of study starting early and continuing through grade 12 and beyond. Furthermore, the vast majority of parents are open to learning about the benefits of a long-sequence foreign language program, and it is the responsibility of foreign language professionals to keep parents informed and involved. Next to foreign language teachers, parents are the most influential members of a community regarding the implementation of standards, and their support or lack of support can make or break a program.

THE LOCAL COMMUNITY AND ITS DECISION MAKERS

More than any other academic subject, foreign language study requires that the community buy into its validity. Often the community is willing to commit resources and tax dollars to education-related programs, but not necessarily to foreign languages. Foreign language educators are often led to believe that "there is no money" for language programs, but the fact is that local communities and their decision-makers have set other programs as higher priorities. Communities have the funds to support a K-12 foreign language curriculum. Nevertheless, for years schools have taken on additional responsibilities that are not true academics, resulting in less funding for the academic programs, notably foreign languages. Because funding plays a major role in the implementation of standards, foreign language teachers need to go the distance to convince those in charge of the purse strings that foreign language study is an integral part of the curriculum and that language study is essential to the academic success of all students.

Foreign language teachers are obligated to advocate for high-quality and long-sequence programs within the community. Effective advocacy involves providing information to, garnering support from, and collaborating with all groups that make up the school and community. An incomplete list of local groups follows:

school building and school district committees, school/community committees (such as strategic planning committees or violence prevention committees), parent teacher organizations, boards of education, businesses (particularly businesses with international ties), Rotary International, Optimists, newspapers, and radio and television stations.

THE STATE AND ITS DECISION MAKERS

In order to advocate on behalf of foreign language education at the state level, foreign language professionals should know how the state meets its responsibility of providing K-12 public education. For example, some state constitutions allow states to mandate curriculum, while others do not. In the states that allow curriculum mandates, it is appropriate for the foreign language profession to lead or become involved in a foreign language mandate. In states that do not allow mandates, other measures need to be taken to ensure that adequate foreign language instruction for all students is in place. Also, it is important to understand the role of professional associations such as the state foreign language association and the state education association, as well as the roles of the department of education, the board of education, and the legislature. Just as importantly, one should become familiar with the interrelationships of the state-level entities that affect foreign language education and education in general. The next step is to learn how to work with these different state-level entities that affect foreign language education policy. In order to achieve the vision of the implementation of standards, a united foreign language profession may have to become more active at the state level.

THE FEDERAL GOVERNMENT,
ITS AGENCIES AND DECISION MAKERS

Successful foreign language programs depend in large part on politics and activities favorable to foreign language education within local, state, regional, and national communities. The United States government will support and contribute funding to programs that our decision-making representatives perceive that U.S. citizens believe to be valuable. Again, foreign language professionals have a civic as well as a professional obligation to send a united message to our senators and congressmen. For many years many have been reluctant to become politically involved and to communicate with our leaders in Washington, D.C. Consequently, foreign language education in the United States generally has taken a back seat, resulting in less than adequate programs. Nonetheless, thanks to the leadership and continuing advocacy efforts of the Joint National Committee for Languages – National Council for Languages and International Studies (JNCL-NCLIS), foreign language education has become and continues to become much more prominent on the national scene.

It is important to remember that the perception of nations around the world concerning America's capabilities of successfully communicating in other languages and of successfully interacting within other cultures also affects the ultimate implementation of standards. In recent years, the federal government has noted that it is critical for national security and in our country's best interests that citizens be able to communicate proficiently beyond U.S. borders. American international businesses and the U.S. Department of Defense—to name just two entities—acknowledge the need for bilingual and multilingual individuals. The only federal program to appropriate funding solely to the creation of foreign language instructional programs (with criteria to include long-sequence programs) is the Foreign Language Assistance Program (FLAP). (See JNCL-NCLIS web site: http://www.languagepolicy.org/.)

All foreign language professionals are charged with the commitment to work towards effecting change that would allow for improved foreign language education to be accessed by students of all ages. Even though local foreign language programs are the function of individual states and local control, the influence of the federal government and its associated agencies plays a vital role in the success of local programs. Fortunately, the recent standards documents present educators with the means to their implementation. For the benefit of students in American schools, foreign language educators with a united message must increase advocacy efforts with the ultimate goal of improved foreign language education.

FACTORS UNIQUE TO THE TEACHING OF SPANISH

Perceptions of the public, including the Hispanic population, regarding the Spanish language and Hispanic cultures greatly affect instructional Spanish programs. Schools often emphasize the importance of Hispanic LEP students learning English, to the exclusion of continued development in Spanish. Hispanic students learn that their language and culture are not valued and respected. Such emphasis on learning English actually decreases the potential of Hispanic students reaching their maximum proficiency level in English. In addition, their opportunities to become literate in Spanish have been greatly reduced, as have their chances of becoming bilingual. Laws at all levels have been passed or attempted, in order to erase the value of Spanish language development for Hispanics. Since Ana Roca treats this topic in depth in Chapter 5 of this volume, it suffices to mention here that Spanish language as well as other foreign language professionals should collaborate with professional associations related to ESL and bilingual or dual language programs to effect the best possible environment in which the implementation of standards can take place.

PROGRAM PLANNING

Information presented in this volume serves as the foundation to plan, develop, and implement K-12 foreign language programs. The focus of this section will be on the planning of a FLES program as part of K-12 foreign language instruction. However, the general steps outlined can be adapted to any proposed program. In order to facilitate the discussion, "Program Planning" has been divided into three phases:

- Phase I: Identification of Program Need
- Phase II: Planning a Long-Sequence Foreign Language Program
- Phase III: Program Implementation

Phase I: Identification of Program Need

The first important step is to obtain an official directive, such as a directive from the local board of education, to study the need for a FLES program. A K-12 foreign language study committee representing a broad cross-section of the community should be formed to include parents, elementary classroom teachers, district foreign language teachers, principals, administrators, professionals and/or business members from the local community, and members representing the board of education. This committee will be charged with 1) researching the benefits of a K-12 program, with an emphasis on a FLES component, 2) researching existing FLES programs to identify available options, 3) presenting and discussing preliminary committee findings with elementary school staffs, parent teacher organizations, building and district accountability committees, etc., 4) surveying individuals who participated in discussions about FLES, and 5) reporting results to the board of education.

Before discussions (step 3 in the above paragraph) take place with school and community groups, the committee should create a mission statement, a rationale, and a set of beliefs for the proposed program. Foreign language teachers in Summit School District RE-1 in Colorado created a document that was eventually included in the introduction to the foreign language curriculum. The sample document follows:

MISSION

The Summit School District RE-1 K-12 Foreign Language program will better prepare individuals to be members of an increasingly complex, interrelated and global society.

RATIONALE

We believe that it is necessary for Summit School District RE-1 to provide a K-12 Foreign Language program for the following reasons:

- To be prepared for the future in our global society, it is essential that Summit students develop and maintain proficiency in more than one language.
- To develop proficiency in more than one language, children need to begin language learning early.
- To improve relations with people from around the world, communication in other languages is imperative.
- To develop a foundation for true understanding and appreciation of international cultures, knowledge of other languages is critical.

BELIEFS

Knowledge of another language:

- Is attainable by all.
- Raises self-esteem.
- Creates a sense of belonging to an interrelated society.
- Increases opportunities in life and work.
- Helps produce citizens who contribute to humanity.

- Develops insights into the learner's own language and culture.
- Enhances sensitivity to our culturally diverse society.

Foreign language study in early childhood:

- Expands children's horizons to the world.
- Increases acceptance of cultural diversity.
- Not only enhances the elementary school curriculum but also is an integral part of it.
- Leads to greater proficiency throughout life.
- Consistently results in higher standardized test scores.
- Develops greater mental flexibility, creativity and critical thinking skills.
- Is the optimum time because children are open to learning new things, lack inhibition and easily acquire foreign language skills.

To build on the above document, it is helpful to create a program vision that provides a sense of direction and is aligned with the district's goals. The program vision for Summit School District RE-1 follows:

> Children will be introduced to Spanish in Kindergarten; Spanish instruction will continue in the elementary classrooms through fifth grade. The K-5 Spanish curriculum will be "content-related." In the middle school, students will have the opportunity to continue their development of Spanish language skills by taking bilingual classes taught in English and Spanish. Furthermore, middle school students will have the option to learn additional languages. In high school, students may take content-area classes in Spanish, or Spanish and English. Also, high school students will have the option to learn additional languages.

Even though the program vision may never be realized in its entirety, it provides a direction and a holistic view of how the program should proceed.

The best manner in which to research existing FLES programs is to visit them, so that committee members have the opportunity to visit with FLES teachers and other school personnel. In addition, articles, books, and other resources, such as the Center for Applied Linguistics in Washington, D.C., should be consulted in order to be in a position to discuss adequately a potential FLES program, and ultimately, to make valid recommendations.

Once the committee has researched existing FLES programs, it is ready to present and discuss the benefits of a FLES program with school/community committees and/or associations, which include PTAs, accountability committees, site-based decision- making committees, and teaching staff. The next step is for those who take part in the FLES discussions to fill out a survey. The cumulative survey results then will serve as hard data when it is time to present the committee's finding to the board of education. It is especially important to survey those who participated in the discussions about FLES, because the committee will want only informed responses. The survey should be brief and to the point. In fact, one question with space for comments is sufficient: "If budgeting and scheduling are not insurmountable, do you support the concept of a K-12 foreign language program? ___yes ___no Comments _____" Even though community groups, such as Rotary International, would not fill out the survey, it is important to inform community groups about the possible expanded foreign language program, in order to obtain buy-in.

Once the study committee has compiled the above information, a presentation to the board of education to request board approval of the proposed program is in order. The presentation should include a history of any previous FLES activities, and presentations from at least one parent, classroom teacher, principal or other administrator, and community member. Results of the survey should be presented, followed by the committee's recommendations concerning the FLES planning and implementation phases. After the board of education approves the FLES proposal, Phase II may begin.

Phase II: Planning a Long-Sequence Foreign Language Program

Adequate planning, of at least one school year prior to the projected initial implementation date, is highly recommended as essential to the success of a program. Staff time should be allocated to work on the planning phase. If a "volunteer" is expected to plan a FLES program on top of teaching full-time, the necessary planning phase is shortchanged. Sufficient planning is key to a successful FLES program.

During Phase II, a FLES curriculum is created, aligned with the district standards, and instructional materials to support the curriculum are researched and acquired. Appropriate assessments are developed. The recruitment of FLES teachers and pre-service training to implement FLES takes place. It is critical that collaborative ties be formed with classroom teachers, administrators and other building and district personnel. Teaching pilot FLES classes is an ideal way for classroom teachers and administrators to experience firsthand what a FLES program will look like in their school. Also, the implementation of a FLES program necessitates the development of a program budget.

It is important to dialogue with district foreign language teachers every step of the way, even after the FLES program begins. Ongoing articulation with middle school and high school foreign language teachers will prove extremely beneficial to a successful K-12 foreign language program. Students will be entering the upper grades with increased language skills, which will necessitate program changes in the middle school and high school.

Parent and community buy-in continues to play a critical role throughout the planning, implementation, and maintenance of a FLES program. Presentations and video clips of the pilot classes to school and community groups helps to cement school and community support of the program. The creation of a foreign language advisory group is wise. This advisory council should consist of a cross-section of the school and community. This group can take on projects such as program evaluation and present findings to administrators and/or the board of education. Public relations activities through the local media go a long way in gathering support for the FLES program. Phase III is on the horizon.

Phase III: Program Implementation

The anticipated FLES program finally begins. In order to implement and maintain a successful FLES program, the activities of the previous two phases will need to remain intact. FLES teachers will require in-service training and general support. Dialogue and articulation within the K-12 foreign language department is again essential. The revision of curriculum and assessments will be ongoing, as will the development of a FLES budget. An active foreign language advisory group will help to ensure that the FLES issues are addressed. Public relations through the media and within the community must also continue. These steps will contribute to the continuation and maintenance of a successful FLES program.

CONCLUSION

Foreign language professionals "envision a future in which ALL students will develop and maintain proficiency in English and at least one other language, modern or classical" (National Standards...Project 1999, 7). All students of all ages should have the opportunity—through a long-sequence program of high-quality instruction—to achieve the standards, resulting in high proficiency in at least one language other than English. The future holds the promise that foreign language professionals have the ability to move foreign language education from the past and current "realities" to the "vision" of all students having the opportunity to achieve the standards at a high proficiency level.

Both negative factors and positive factors can be identified that affect the implementation of standards. Defeatist attitudes will severely stunt the progress of learning. In fact, research has demonstrated that foreign language learning is attainable by all, raises self-esteem, increases overall academic performance in school, and contributes to increased proficiency in the basic skills. However, the philosophy that foreign language study is for all students, not just college-bound, above-average, motivated students, has posed challenges to foreign language educators. The fact that diverse students with special needs are welcome in all classrooms is an acknowledgement that foreign language educators are seeking out eclectic methods that coincide with language acquisition theories. Diverse students, including heritage learners, often serve as valuable resources to our classrooms and communities.

In order to progress in the direction of student achievement of standards, the foreign language profession is in the process of transformation. Teachers are learning more about language acquisition at all ages, including among FLES students; are willing and able to adapt teaching and instructional programs to reflect individual differences in their students; and are realizing the importance of articulation among all levels of instruction, K-16. Language educators also are aware of the importance of collaborating with non-foreign language school and district staff to achieve the goal of the realization of standards. They know the professional value of being active members in professional associations of AATSP, ACTFL, regional and state foreign language associations. The National Board for Professional Teaching Standards for Foreign Language Teachers document (forthcoming) outlines the teaching standards that teachers need in order to help students achieve the student standards.

Members of local, state, national, and multilingual/multicultural communities and their decision-makers greatly affect the implementation of standards. More and more parents are supporting long-sequence and high-quality foreign language programs as an integral part of the school curriculum. Local community buy-in is critical to the success of foreign language programs. Just as important is that foreign language educators work within their individual states to effect favorable changes. It is also essential that our leaders in Washington, D.C., hear from the foreign language profession. Support and financial resources are made available to programs that elected officials perceive to be valued by their constituents. Therefore, it is the responsibility of the foreign language profession to communicate a united message.

The vision of standards implementation necessitates that long-sequence foreign language programs be planned, developed, implemented, and maintained. A strong rationale for expanded foreign language programs currently exists. The challenge is that all students of all ages be provided foreign language instruction as an integral part of the school curriculum.

WORKS CITED

Begley, Sharon. "Your Child's Brain." *Newsweek* February 19, 1996:55-62.

Boston, Carol. "Federal Support for Foreign Language Education." *ERIC Review* 6, 1 (1998): 42-6.

Curtain, Helena and Carol Ann Pesola. *Languages and Children: Making the Match.* 2nd ed. White Plains, NY: Longman, 1994.

De Houwer, Annick. "Two or More Languages in Early Childhood: Some General Points and Practical Recommendations." ERIC Digest. Washington, D.C.: Center for Applied Linguistics, July 1999.

National Standards in Foreign Language Education Project. *Standards for Foreign Language Learning in the 21st Century.* Lawrence, KS: Allen, 1999.

Olkin, Jacqueline. National Board for Professional Teaching Standards. Personal Communication, January 2000.

Rafferty, Eileen. *Second Language Study and Basic Skills in Louisiana.* Baton Rouge, LA: Louisiana Department of Education 1986. [EDRS ED 283 360]

Robinson, Deborah Wilburn. "The Cognitive, Academic, and Attitudinal Benefits of Early Language Learning." *Critical Issues in Early Second Language Learning: Building for Our Children's Future.* Ed. Myriam Met. Glenview, IL: Scott-Foresman Addison-Wesley, 1998. 37-42.

Shrum, Judith L., and Eileen W. Glisan. *Teacher's Handbook.* 2nd ed. Boston: Heinle & Heinle, 2000: 254-90.

Voght, Geoffrey M. and Christine Uber Grosse. "The Development of Spanish and Portuguese for Specific Purposes in the United States." *Spanish and Portuguese for Business and the Professions.* Eds. T. Bruce Fryer and Gail Guntermann. Lincolnwood, IL: National Textbook Co., 1998. 3-22.

Woodford, Protase. "Making a World of Difference—Children and Languages in North Carolina" (video). Matthew, SC: CIN Services, Inc., 1991. (P.O. Box 1670).

APPENDIX A
STANDARDS FOR LEARNING SPANISH

Goal 1 Communication
Communicate in Spanish

Standard 1.1 Students engage in conversation, provide and obtain information, express feelings and emotions, and exchange opinions.

Standard 1.2 Students understand and interpret written and spoken Spanish on a variety of topics.

Standard 1.3 Students present information, concepts, and ideas in Spanish to an audience of listeners or readers on a variety of topics.

Goal 2 Culture
Gain Knowledge and Understanding of Spanish-Speaking Cultures

Standard 2.1 Students demonstrate an understanding of the relationship between the practices and perspectives of Hispanic cultures.

Standard 2.2 Students demonstrate an understanding of the relationship between the products and perspectives of Hispanic cultures.

Goal 3 Connections
Connect with Other Disciplines and Acquire Information

Standard 3.1 Students reinforce and further their knowledge of other disciplines through Spanish.

Standard 3.2 Students acquire information and recognize the distinctive viewpoints that are available only through the Spanish language and its cultures.

Goal 4 Comparisons
Develop Insights into the Nature of Language and Culture

Standard 4.1 Students demonstrate understanding of the nature of language through comparisons between Spanish and English.

Standard 4.2 Students demonstrate understanding of the concept of culture through comparisons between Hispanic cultures and their own.

Goal 5 Communities
Participate in Multilingual Communities at Home and Around the World

Standard 5.1 Students use Spanish both within and beyond the school setting.

Standard 5.2 Students show evidence of becoming life-long learners by using Spanish for personal enjoyment and enrichment.

APPENDIX B
SELECTED ADDITIONAL RESOURCES

BOOKS AND ARTICLES

Allen, Linda Quinn. "Designing Curriculum for Standards-Based Culture/Language Learning." *NECTFL Review* 47 (Spring 2000):14-21.

American Association of Departments of Foreign Languages. "Forum on the Standards For Foreign Language Learning." *ADFL Bulletin* 31.1 (1999): 70-87.

Amores, María J., and Frank W. Medley, Jr. "From Rhetoric to Reality: Applying AATSP Standards to the Spanish Classroom." *Dimension '98: Communications, Cultures, Connections, Comparisons, Communities.* Proceedings of the 1998 Southern Conference on Language Teaching. Valdosta, GA: SCOLT Publications, 1998. 1-18.

Biron, Christina. "Bringing Standards to Life: Points of Departure." *Foreign Language Annals* 31.4 (1998): 584-94.

Gifford, Charlotte, and Jeanne Mullaney. "From Rhetoric to Reality: Applying the Communication Standards to the Classroom." *NECTFL Review* 46 (Fall 1999): 12-18.

Harper, Jane, Madeleine Lively, and Mary Williams, eds. *The Coming of Age of the Profession.* Boston: Heinle & Heinle, 1998.

International Society for Technology in Education. *National Educational Technology Standards for students: Connecting Curriculum and Technology.* Eugene, OR: ISTE, 2000. http://cnets.iste.org

Jackson, Claire W., ed. *A Challenge to Change: The Language Learning Continuum.* New York: The College Entrance Examination Board, 1999.

Jackson, Claire W., et al. *Articulation and Achievement: Connecting Standards, Performance, and Assessment in Foreign Language.* New York: The College Entrance Examination Board, 1996.

Lafayette, Robert C., ed. *National Standards: A Catalyst for Reform.* ACTFL Foreign Language Education Series. Lincolnwood, IL: National Textbook Co., 1996.

Lally, Caroly. "Using the National Standards to Improve Foreign Language Articulation: An Alternative to Placement Exams." *Dimension '98.* 93-100.

Marzano, Robert J., and John S. Kendall. *A Comprehensive Guide to Designing Standards- Based Districts, Schools, and Classrooms.* Aurora, CO: Mid- Continental Regional Educational Laboratory (McREL), 1996.

Met, Myriam. "Foreign Language Curriculum in an Era of Educational Reform." *Content of the Curriculum.* 2nd ed. Ed. Allan Glatthorn. Alexandria, VA: Association for Supervision and Curriculum Development, 1995. 69-98.

_____. "Foreign Language Instruction in Middle Schools: A New View for the Coming Century." *Foreign Language Learning: The Journey of a Lifetime.* Eds. Richard Donato and Robert M. Terry. Lincolnwood, IL: National Textbook Co., 1995. 76-109.

_____. "Making Connections." *Foreign Language Standards: Linking Theory, Research, and Practice.* Ed. June K. Phillips. Lincolnwood, IL: National Textbook Co., 1999. 137-64.

National K-12 Foreign Language Resource Center. *Bringing the Standards into the Classroom: A Teacher's Guide.* Ames, IA: Iowa State University, 1997.

Packard, Craig, and Lynn Fischer. "Journals and Newsletters." (List of addresses.) *ERIC Review* 6.1 (Fall 1998): 56-7.

Phillips, June K., ed. *Foreign Language Standards: Linking Research, Theories, and Practice.* ACTFL Foreign Language Education Series. Lincolnwood, IL: National Textbook Co., 1999.

_____, ed. *Collaborations: Meeting New Goals, New Realities.* Northeast Conference Reports. Lincolnwood, IL: National Textbook Co., 1997.

Sandrock, Paul. *State Standards: Connecting a National Vision to Local Implementation.* ACTFL White Paper/Professional Issues Report. Yonkers, NY: American Council on the Teaching of Foreign Languages, 1997.

Smith, Alfred N. "Designing a Standards-Based Thematic Unit Using the Learning Scenario As an Organizing Framework." *ACTFL Newsletter* 11.3 (Spring 1999): 9-12.

Swender, Elvira, and Greg Duncan. "ACTFL Performance Guidelines for K-12 Learners." *Foreign Language Annals* 31.4 (1998): 479-91.

Terry, Robert M., ed. *Agents of Change in a Changing Age.* Northeast Conference Reports. Lincolnwood, IL: National Textbook Co., 2000.

Wiggins, Grant. Educative Assessment: Designing Assessments to Inform and Improve Student Performance. San Francisco: Jossey-Bass, 1998.

Winston, Laurel, and Lynn Fischer. "Foreign Language Resource Organizations." (Addresses of professional organizations, conferences, and language resource centers.) *ERIC Review* 6.1 (Fall 1998): 46-53.

_____ and Craig Packard. "Books." (List of resources for language teachers.) *ERIC Review* 6.1 (Fall 1998): 53-5.

WORLD WIDE WEB SITES

ERIC/CLL Resource Guides:
   http://www.cal.org/ericcll/faqs/rgos/sns.htm

ERIC Review:
   http://www.accesseric.org/resources/ericreview/review.html

LangNet (Compilation of resources for specific learner profiles, under
   development by National Foreign Language Center):
   http://www.nflc.org/projects/langnet.asp

Putnam Valley (NY) BOCES:
   http://putwest.boces.org/Standards.html

VIDEOS

American Association of Teachers of Spanish and Portuguese. "Spanish
   and Portuguese in the Twenty-First Century." AATSP, 1999.

Northeast Conference on the Teaching of Foreign Languages.
   "Collaborations: Meeting New Goals, New Realities." Northeast
   Conference, 1997.

ADDRESSES

Allen Press (to order national standards):
National Standards Project
P.O. Box 1897
Lawrence, KS 66044

Tel. 913-843-1221

American Association of Teachers of Spanish and Portuguese (AATSP)
Lynn A Sandstedt, Executive Director
Butler-Hancock 210
University of Northern Colorado
Greeley, CO 80639

Tel. 970-351-1090
E-mail: AATSP@bentley.unco.edu
Web site: http://www.aatsp.org/

American Council on the Teaching of Foreign Languages (ACTFL)
6 Executive Plaza
Yonkers, NY 10701-6801

Tel. 914-963-8830
E-mail: actflhq@aol.com
Web site: http://www.actfl.org/

Association of Departments of Foreign Languages (ADFL)
10 Astor Place
New York, NY 10003-6981

Tel. 212-614-6320
E-mail: elizabeth.welles@mla.org
Web site: http://www.adfl.org/

Center for Advanced Research on Language Acquisition (CARLA)
University of Minnesota
333 Appleby hall
128 Pleasant St. S.E.
Minneapolis, MN 55455

Tel. 612-626-8600
E-mail: carla@tc.umn.edu
Web site: http://carla.acad.umn.edu/

Center for Applied Linguistics and ERIC/CLL
4646 40th Street, NW
Washington, D.C. 20016-1859

Tel. 800-276-9834
E-mail: eric@cal.org
Web site: http://www.cal.org/ericcll/

Center for Language Education and Research (CLEAR)
Michigan State University
A712 Wells Hall
East Lansing, MI 48824-1027

Tel. 517-432-2286
E-mail: clear@msu.edu
Web site: http://clear.msu.edu/

Central States Conference on the Teaching of Foreign Languages
(CSCFLT)
2801 S. University
Little Rock, AR 72204

Tel. 501-569-8159
E-mail: rmcheatham@ualr.edu
Web site: http://www.ualr.edu/~centralstate/

Joint National Committee for Languages (JNCL)
4646 40th Street, NW
Washington, D.C. 20016-1859

Tel. 202-966-8477
E-mail: info@languagepolicy.org
Web site: http://www.languagepolicy.org/jncl.html

Language Acquisition Resource Center (LARC)
San Diego State University
5500 Campanile Drive, BAM 424
San Diego, CA 92182-7703

Tel. 619-594-6177
E-mail: nlrcsd@mail.sdsu.edu
Web site: http://larcnet.sdsu.edu/

National Capital Language Resource Center (NCLRC)
2600 Virginia Ave., NW
Suite 105
Washington, DC 20037

Tel. 202-739-0607
E-mail: nclrc@nicom.com
Web site: http://www.cal.org/nclrc/

The National Foreign Language Center
at The University of Maryland (NFLC) (for LangNet)
1029 Vermont Avenue, 10th Floor
Washington, DC 20005

Tel. 202-637-8881
Web site: http://www.nflc.org/projects/langnet.asp

National Foreign Language Resource Center (NFLRC)
University of Hawai'i at Manoa
1859 East-West Road #106
Honolulu, Hawai'i 96822

Tel. 808-956-9424
E-mail: nflrc@hawaii.edu
Web site: http://www.LLL.hawaii.edu/nflrc/

National K-12 Foreign Language Resource Center (NFLRC)
Iowa State University
N131 Lagomarcino Hall
Ames, IA 50011

Tel. 515-294-6699
E-mail: nflrc@iastate.edu
Web site: http://www.educ.iastate.edu/nflrc/

Northeast Conference on the Teaching of Foreign Languages (NECTFL)
The Northeast Conference at Dickinson College
P.O. Box 1773
College and Louther Streets
Carlisle, PA 17013-2896

Tel. 717-245-1977
E-mail: nectfl@dickinson.edu
Web site: http://www.dickinson.edu/nectfl/

Southern Conference on Language Teaching (SCOLT)
165 Lazy Laurel Chase
Roswell, GA 30076

Tel. 770-992-1256
E-mail: Lynnemcc@mindspring.com
Web site: http://www.valdosta.edu/scolt/

SCOLT Publications
Valdosta State University
Valdosta, GA 31698

Tel. 912-333-7358

Southwest Conference on Language Teaching (SWCOLT)
1348 Coachman Dr.
Sparks, NV 89434

FAX: 702-358-1605
E-mail: acournia@compuserve.com
